Tracking Down Your Ancestors

If you want to know how . . .

Improving Your Written English
*Ensure your grammar, punctuation and spelling
are up to scratch*

Writing Your Life Story
*How to record and present your memories for
future generations to enjoy*

Say it with Pictures
*Apply graphical communications to transform
your personal effectiveness*

Times of Our Lives
The essential companion for writing your own life story

Meet Your Ancestors

Please send for a free copy of the latest catalogue:

How To Books
3 Newtec Place, Magdalen Road,
Oxford OX4 1RE, United Kingdom
email: info@howtobooks.co.uk
http://www.howtobooks.co.uk

Tracking Down Your Ancestors

Discover the story behind your ancestors and bring your family history to life

DR HARRY ALDER

howtobooks

Special thanks to Else Churchill, a genealogist and director of the Society of Genealogists (www.sog.org.uk) for her help with technical editing.

Published by How To Books Ltd,
3 Newtec Place, Magdalen Road,
Oxford OX4 1RE. United Kingdom.
Tel: (01865) 793806. Fax: (01865) 248780.
email: info@howtobooks.co.uk
http://www.howtobooks.co.uk

First published 2002
Reprinted 2003
Reprinted 2005

British Library Cataloguing in Publication Data
A catalogue record for this book is available from the British Library

Cover design by Baseline Arts Ltd, Oxford
Produced for How To Books by Deer Park Productions, Tavistock
Typeset by Dorwyn Ltd, Rowlands Castle, Hants
Printed and bound by Cromwell Press, Trowbridge, Wiltshire

NOTE: The material contained in this book is set out in good faith for general guidance and no liability can be accepted for loss or expense incurred as a result of relying in particular circumstances on statements made in the book. The laws and regulations are complex and liable to change, and readers should check the current position with the relevant authorities before making personal arrangements.

Contents

Appendices

Abbreviations

The following are some common abbreviations I have used throughout the book:

AGRA	Association of Genealogists & Record Agents
BDMs	Births, Deaths and Marriages
BigR	British Isles Genealogical Register
BTs	Bishops' Transcripts
CRO	County Record Office
FH	Family History
FFHS	Federation of Family History Societies
FHC	Family History Centre (of LDS), also known as FHL (FH Library)
FHS	Family History Society
FRC	Family Records Centre
GOONS	Guild of One-Name Studies
GRO	General Register Office
IGI	International Genealogical Index
LDS	Church of Jesus Christ of Latter-day Saints
MI	Monumental Inscriptions
ONS	Office of National Statistics
PRO	Public Record Office
SoG	Society of Genealogists

Introduction

Millions of people around the world spend time, energy and money tracking down dead relatives. In the vast majority of cases these enthusiasts are ordinary people, direct or indirect descendants, with a personal rather than professional interest. As a hobby, it seems this gives a lot of pleasure over a long period.

'Family history research' is said to be the fastest growing hobby in the UK, as well as being the second most popular topic on the internet. Tracing ancestors has been especially popular in the USA since the days of the epochal Alex Hailey film and novel *Roots*. It seems to go deeper than your average hobby, fulfilling some sort of basic need to get to know our origins and, presumably, understand ourselves better in the process. It can certainly throw up some great stories, quotable even outside your own family circle, and provide no end of fun and pleasure.

Based on the number of generations we have clocked up in a few centuries, and the remarkable effect of compound growth, we all have recorded ancestors in plenty. It seems that statistically even the most anonymous of 21st century families are the progeny of a motley congregation of the good, great, sick, sad, strange, evil, infamous and interestingly mediocre. Like leaves on a summer tree, those early branches (we must come from somewhere) soon make big numbers, harbouring more Toms and Marys, let alone thieves and paupers, than you would have thought a respectable family tree could bear. Each Tom and Mary has a story, as rich and unique as yours or mine. Most – let's be realistic – are lost for ever, as their history depends on written records, and back beyond a certain point they could neither read nor write. That loss is sad, however ordinary they were. Some, however, because of our rich genealogical resources and the internet, can be tracked down across the centuries. In a sense that true family historians know well, these people can be made to live again. That's a privilege for them and us, their space age descendants.

Tracking down your ancestors can involve family history, genealogy or both. What's the distinction?

♦ Genealogy usually refers to recording your family tree, or pedigree, as far back as you can go, over one or more family names.
♦ Family history, on the other hand, puts the people you find into their historical context and the aim is to find out as much about them and their contemporary history as possible – their stories.

The history or story part is what makes it addictively interesting.

Look at it this way. Family history research tends to take you off horizontally, exploring the historical context. A single person may be researched in as much detail as the records reveal. Genealogy, however, goes vertically down a top to bottom hierarchy, and is more concerned with the chronology and vital events. It deals much with names and dates and although it can be very challenging, when compared to family history it has been likened to train-spotting. That's unfair, as who will not get some satisfaction when they prove a direct family line going back maybe to the time of Shakespeare? But most people intuitively want to know much more about their ancestors, even if just in respect of a few of them. For example:

◆ What did they die of?
◆ Did any of them emigrate?
◆ Where to and how did their lives change?
◆ Were any transported – or hanged? For what offence?
◆ Are there distant cousins today in other parts of the world – or across town?
◆ Were any ancestors famous – or infamous?
◆ Any juicy crimes in that innocuous genealogical pedigree?
◆ Paupers? Workhouse inmates?
◆ What about their trades or professions – even titles?
◆ Any fortunes made during the industrial revolution?
◆ What's the record number of children (a) born and (b) that lived to adulthood?
◆ How about recurrent twins over the generations?
◆ What Christian names predominated?
◆ Did any hit the local newspapers – 15 minutes of fame?

Family history is replete with stories of your own folk that will bring them to life in fascinating and often extraordinary ways.

Widespread use of computers and internet access has added to a more recent spurt in the growth of what is now an industry. However, as we shall see, you cannot get very far if you limit yourself to the internet. But it is a catalyst, and attracts those who might never get started on the orthodox genealogical route. You can still have plenty of fun and, depending on your surname and what has been done already, you may strike it lucky in ancestral cyberspace.

The US leads the way in family history as a serious hobby. Americans are probably better represented in research into UK, 'old country' ancestry than UK residents themselves. So, although some of the top websites are US biased, they none the less have plenty of content about British ancestry, useful to British researchers. The UK is certainly blessed with a wealth of archived material housed in public records offices and libraries, stretching back to the Norman conquest. Anyone prepared to delve into a little Latin and Old English and expand their school history can search these very early dates – if not there is no end of help available. This is attractive to many thousands of new world descendants of the islands – including Australians – who have no less affinity with their Anglo Saxon roots than natives and whose ranks have fuelled the growth of family history to its present popularity.

Most of the material the serious hobbyist will wish to explore in public record offices is accessible either free of charge or at a nominal cost if you can go to the location of the records. So it need not be an a expensive activity. It is the sheer diversity and detail of information about our ancestors, in addition to the increasing accessibility of records of births, deaths and marriages, that makes for such a rewarding hobby.

The Church of Jesus Christ of Latter-Day Saints (LDS) has probably had the single greatest influence on the growth of genealogy and family history as an amateur activity. They have their own special reasons connected with proxy baptism for ancestors, but they have made their staggeringly large databases open to the public through their Family History Centres, the central library at Salt Lake City, Utah and the FamilySearch website. Family History Centres are located in towns throughout the country and anyone can use them. LDS members have contributed a large part of the International Genealogical Index (IGI), a major surname index of parish records, accessible online as well as at Family History Centres.

Most readers will have access to a computer, and probably the internet, and this is increasingly likely as usage continues to grow. In the case of a hobby like family history, help from within the family is also more likely, and young computer whiz kid relatives are usually ready to display their talents. For readers considering going online, the attractions of family history and the benefits of online resources may be enough to tip the balance and justify the decision. Having said that, we shall see that you certainly cannot rely solely on the internet to do serious family research, as it does not give access to primary, or original records upon which reliable research must be based.

But what the computer does well, it does very well. At minimum, it can save you a lot of time, effort and expense. In particular, important genealogical data is gradually being indexed and made freely available through the internet. This can help to point you in the right direction, both in terms of the availability and nature or content of the records you need, and – through world wide web searching – whether they contain a reference to your family name.

Perhaps most of all, the internet offers access to literally millions of people with similar interests. There is a spirit of sharing and mutual support that cannot be compared with the support you might get in more traditional research, other than very locally in a family history society. Through email lists and newsgroups, communication is also very fast, so help is more or less on demand around the clock. Another big advantage is access to research already carried out that may be accessible only through the internet. In other words, somebody may have already researched all or part of your own family line, and what you can download in minutes may represent many years of painstaking work. The internet offers therefore a worldwide clearing house for such data, offering obvious mutual benefits. This usually affects the *genealogical* (family trees or pedigrees) more than *family history* nature of research. You can then devote your attention to what for most people is the more interesting and rewarding, hands-on aspect of the hobby – getting to know your ancestors through the diverse types of records that exist. After a few 'hits', in practice it is rare to get very far using just the internet. So you will not be spared the necessary experience of more conventional spadework, and the obstacles and frustration that accompany it. In the long run this is for the best.

With sensible planning, the hobby need not involve much expense. In many cases you can obtain information by post in far less time and at lower cost than travelling up and down the country. For many, however, travel – such as to old church graveyards, houses and places connected with individual ancestors, and at some impressive libraries – adds an extra dimension and more pleasure. Except for a few visits to record offices that may be almost obligatory – especially to make a good start – you have the choice about how mobile or sedentary an interest you want to pursue. You have a similar choice in the way you conduct your research when collecting, at the outset, information from living relatives.

Family history can be anything you want it to be. For instance, a one-off project, a lifetime hobby, or a bit of fun. You can approach it at any level, from deadly serious to 100 per cent leisure mode – or a healthy mixture. Likewise, it can be highly technical and mentally demanding, or a therapeutic alternative to your main line of work. Having said that, it may not finish up the way it starts. Family history research tends to evolve and grow in a person's life as their knowledge and skills increase, and as they experience its unique pleasures and challenges. Hence often an increasing enthusiasm over the months and years, and pleasure from time to time bordering on euphoria as you make surprising discoveries. A caveat: commitment leading to straight addiction is not unknown.

Chapter 1 gets you off to a start without getting stuck, losing interest or spending unnecessary time, energy and money. The tips and guidelines are with a view to a long-term interest rather than a flash-in-the-pan genealogical excursion. In Chapter 2, I describe two main websites where you can do early family name searching and pick up a lot of basic help in the process. Many other websites are equally useful but either cover similar ground or are for more specialised purposes. You will probably need to do some conventional digging in local public record offices before reverting to these later in your research, and wider online resources feature later in the book also. This chapter allows you to taste the internet resources straight away and hopefully find a few ancestors that somebody else has already taken an interest in. From the main sources featured in Chapter 2 you can also print or download helpful guides and articles so you can programme your own pace of DIY learning. A single book cannot begin to tap what is out there, and an aim of this book is to get you off to a good start so that you can progress as far as you wish under your own steam.

As with most topics on the internet – and very few topics are not represented – a handful of sites cater for maybe 80 to 90 per cent of what you will need, and even these repeat and overlap information. Thereafter your needs will probably be more specialised, such as geographically, by name, or in the kind of research you happen to be doing at the time. So the book introduces a variety of representative websites, including those hosted by genealogical organisations and the main public record offices.

Some of the most popular sites are very large, having grown by the contributions of ordinary people adding information and 'links'. Much of a site comprises hyperlinks to other useful sites. This is fine, as invariably you will need to get to sites covering more specialised topics or localities as the need arises. But size means that even the site index, or menu, can take some getting to grips with and we cover this, as well as using internet resources generally, in Chapter 3.

The motley sources represented, as well as the size, also present their own problems in terms of the quality and accuracy of data, so it is as well to be sceptical and cautious, and this theme recurs throughout the book. When doing specific online name searches, don't be too disappointed if you draw a blank. The indices are far from complete, although they are gradually being added to by volunteer family historians around the world. If you do locate an ancestor, hold off your celebration until you corroborate the data either from different secondary sources or from original records you access at local records offices. Don't depend on either accuracy (of transcription, say), validity (of the source or an interpretation) or completeness of data drawn from a website. You will appreciate this caveat for yourself all too soon, but it is as well to be forewarned. By history or 'stories' of your ancestors I don't mean straight fiction.

Apart from using a personal computer, a few basic skills are useful, and a little foundational knowledge. Chapter 3 covers the various internet resources that can make for an easy life once you get to know and use them. Chapter 4 concentrates on the important task of transcribing information from original documents to create a dependable database and, if you wish, a worthwhile publication of your good work. Chapter 5 introduces some of the organisations, such as the Society of Genealogists, that hold their own extensive archives and will probably play a big part in your activities. These are no less than a treasure trove of information that may include some of your own ancestors waiting to be found.

Much of your research will involve records of births, deaths and marriages rather than knighthoods, hangings or nine o'clock news items. Chapter 6 explains all about the so-called 'vital' records, which include also parish registers of baptisms, marriages and burials, as well as regular censuses.

Older records can sometimes appear like a foreign language and Chapter 7 focuses on these especially. This covers meanings that can be misleading, abbreviations, and the norms and idiosyncrasies of earlier times. Chapter 8 opens up doors to all manner of record types that can start to put flesh on the skeleton of your family tree and bring your ancestors to life. These are non-vital public records that may reveal the personal, family history facts that your searching is all about. This aspect of family history research reveals another world, to be sure, especially to younger researchers. But given commitment and enthusiasm, that world, and its citizens that held your name, is within your reach, just waiting to be discovered.

1

Getting Started

It is important to make the right start. There is more scope to do silly things, exert unnecessary effort and incur unnecessary expense in family history research as compared with many other hobbies. One false turn can have you barking up the wrong family tree. The internet itself, and what appears like a door to the ultimate instant family pedigree, doesn't help in FH start up mode. Expectations are usually too high, but the world wide web cannot tell you what the older members of your family can. Hence the rule: start with what you know, or can find out from people still alive. In its place, however, the internet can add a lot, even from the start, and especially for those readers who are already familiar with web browsing and online research.

Having said that, making mistakes is an important part of any learning process, and is part of making a good start to anything worthwhile. It is a matter of degree. People often forfeit a lifetime of pleasure in a particular pastime or sport because of a bad start – a poor teacher, bad advice, disparaging comments and so on. The type of mistake also matters – some mistakes are best avoided completely. This chapter sets the starting scene and will hopefully make your early endeavours both effective and enjoyable.

There are a few simple principles, about half a dozen more specific rules, and a tip or two but these amount to no more than common sense. At one level you need to decide what you are most interested in – 'goal setting' and all that – such as genealogy or family history as we have already defined them. Or you may have more specific aims within one or both of these approaches, such as relating to ancestors who fought in certain wars, those who emigrated to the USA, Canada or Australia, or those who share your first name. These decisions impinge on:

◆ the time you want to give
◆ support or at least passive tolerance from within the family
◆ how serious you are about either doing a worthwhile one-off project or establishing an ongoing pastime
◆ present interests, such as history or the military
◆ a desire to leave something unique and of value to your own descendants.

At another level you may just wish to give it a go and see what takes your fancy when you are in a better position to make longer-term decisions. That's fine, and your aims, although important to clarify if you are to do anything seriously and over a long period, can wait a while. Anyway, guidance on setting your aims is part of these Getting Started guidelines.

Most family historians do a regular family tree study. You will probably want to see how far back you can trace your ancestors – say on your father's side. There is a certain 'something' about searching for your own surname a few centuries back – that's the genealogy side. And this is maybe to do with not knowing what you might find, and the surprise when you find it – the real life stories you will inevitably uncover. That's the family history side. Few readers will not want to know *something* about their ancestors, and bring them to life as we discussed in the introduction. In fact you can take both approaches – you need a branch or two of genealogical tree anyway on which to hang your stories. That's what these Getting Started tips and guidelines will prepare you for.

WHAT DO YOU KNOW?

Start with what you know. Draw a simple family tree showing your grandparents, parents, yourself and your children. Add birth, marriage and death dates. Ask older relatives for information until you have got as far into the past as possible. Target your oldest relatives. Write to or telephone those living at a distance. Get to those you don't usually hear from as there is more chance of finding something new (rather than Nan's same old stories). Great aunts and uncles are a potential gold mine. Siblings of grandparents and great-grandparents usually provide more new information. Recollections of childhood and family intelligence can vary a lot, but it pays to get it all recorded anyway. Contemporary friends, neighbours and work colleagues of your oldest relatives can also usually contribute. They may have seen much more of them than the family.

Relative terminology

You will meet different versions of family tree layouts, and you will soon get familiar with showing relationships graphically. Fortunately there are not too many technical terms to learn and most of the words are those in everyday speech. However, it is perhaps worth listing the terms used universally for blood and marriage relationships, as a simple misunderstanding in this particular subject can bring quite disproportionate headaches.

Blood relatives

uncle – the brother of your father or mother
aunt – the sister of your father or mother
sibling – your brother or sister
cousin – the son or daughter of your uncle or aunt
second cousin – the son or daughter of your parents' first cousin
nephew – the son of your brother or sister
niece – the daughter of your brother or sister
grandfather – the father of your father or mother
grandmother – the mother of your father or mother
grandson – your child's son
granddaughter – your child's daughter
great grandfather – the father of one of your grandparents
great grandmother – the mother of one of your grandparents
great uncle – the uncle of one of your parents
great aunt – the aunt of one of your parents

To add an ancestor further back than great grandparent, just add another 'great' for each generation, ad infinitum (or at least A.D. 1066).

Marriage relatives

father-in-law – the father of your spouse
mother-in-law – the mother of your spouse

step-son – the son of your spouse's former marriage

step-daughter - the daughter of your spouse's former marriage

step-mother – your father's second (or subsequent) wife

step-father – your mother's second (or subsequent) husband

half-brother – the male offspring from the remarriage of one of your parents

half-sister – the female offspring from the remarriage of one of your parents

Vital abbreviations

Symbols are also used widely, and although you will come across these soon enough, it is as well to create the right habits when making notes from your initial family research.

b. born

bapt. baptised

= married

(2) second marriage

m. married

d. died

bur. buried

From the outset, as well as getting names and approximate dates, gather any other interesting information, such as about occupations, interests, where your ancestors lived, when they moved and so on. Keep your enquiries open ended ('what was she like as a person') once you have got specific event, date and place questions answered. Ask to be informed of anything else that comes to mind later. Once you are known to be the family record repository it gets easier.

Making history

This is the sort of information you are after:

- names of children, spouse, parents, siblings, and other family members
- birth or baptism, marriage, and death or burial information
- dates of other important events such as emigration or relocation to another part of the country
- age at the time of events
- place or street of residence
- occupations and employers such as hospitals, companies, public authorities
- schools and colleges attended
- military service
- religious affiliations
- town, county or place of origin
- stories, gossip, family legend.

The sorts of documents you need to be on the lookout for are:

- old letters
- journals and diaries
- a family bible
- certificates
- photographs
- copies of records, such as baptism, birth, and marriage
- military papers
- newspaper cuttings and articles.

You may not be the first family sleuth. Find out if anyone in the family has done any sort of ancestor searching before.

Often at least one person in an extended family takes an interest, even if it is just tracking down specific ancestors or acting as the guardian of old family documents, photos or a family bible. Old diaries may turn out to be priceless.

Precious stories

Whatever your eventual aims in tracking down your ancestors it usually helps if you start off in this way. Get as much readily available information as possible on both sides of your family even though your main objective is to research your father's side surname. Jot it all down in a bound notebook or diary so that nothing gets lost. You don't know what you may finish up doing in your FH exploits, and easily obtainable information may take on special value in the future – to others as well as yourself. Domestic investigation is good practice for the research skills you will need at an increasing level. If it involves a bit of detective work, even better. We will cover your specific aims shortly, but the idea is to make a hands-on start and gather all the information you can, which might well influence what you do thereafter. This is a standard, boring rule but it does pay dividends and you will probably have fun doing it. Make a start, anyway. All too soon older relatives die off and precious stories are lost forever.

If you can locate a family bible or similar multi-generational chronicle you may well find ready-made dates and relationships – that's a novice genealogist's holy grail. You may have to politely contact relations to whom you have never given the time of day for a decade or two. This is an ideal reason other than weddings and funerals to keep in touch. Let's face it, if you are to spend time contacting eighteenth century dead relatives you should perhaps give a little attention to living ones.

Old letters may also contain treasures of information so it will help to find out who are the inveterate writers as well as hoarders in the family. You don't have to read them, or boxes of papers dumped on you, all at once, but they may add important information later in your searching. You may be able to take copies and return the originals. Most people hoard newspaper cuttings and anything concerning special events in the lives of family members. Relatives who have lived in the same house for many years will be a good bet as we tend to throw things out on successive house moves. Bear in mind also that old documents tend to stay with the parents rather than go with children when they leave home. Even when families move around a lot, there is usually one sentimental hoarder who guards very personal records. Others will have a mine of information in their head and your job is to extract and record it accurately and objectively. The chances are you will unearth family facts of which your parents knew nothing. You may have set your goal on 1066 and all that, but it's best to start right where you are, verify each stage in the generational tree, and work backwards.

WHO DO YOU KNOW?

In parallel with gleaning all the family intelligence, there are other things you can do to get started. Join a local family history society. You can get details on several of the main internet sites covered later and from the Federation of Family History Societies (Useful Addresses at Appendices 2 and 4). Otherwise refer to a telephone directory or ask at your local reference library. In this way you can pick up any amount of general information and probably get specific help. For many people, this sort of social contact – regardless of the learning benefit and the time and effort it might save – is a large part of the pleasure. You can make friends among the living as well as getting to know the dead.

There is usually particular affinity with family historians with your own surname, and the sooner you make contact the better. These are more likely to be in the local society in the county or town where your ancestral searching leads. Next best is someone in a society *researching* your surname because of a marriage link. You may get even more help by joining distant societies than in the town where you are living. You can make contact over the internet by email, newsgroups and the world wide web and we cover this specifically in Chapter 3. Having the same name bridges all sorts of social barriers and individual differences. You have one important thing in common. More so if you establish a link, even to a very distant living cousin. Blood, they say, is thicker than water.

If you are not bothered about the social side of family history, bear in mind that you will inevitably get stuck somewhere along the line and it pays to have a human source of help in addition to internet websites and professional organisations. Further down the line, you may want to share your own work by email with individuals around the world who are researching the same roots, and who may turn out to be distant cousins and invite you to holiday on their ranch.

WHAT DO YOU WANT?

Decide what you want. For example:

- to produce a family history complete with photographs and interesting information
- to chronicle the earliest ancestors on your father's or mother's side
- to find brains, enterprise, sporting acumen or whatever
- to have a retirement hobby.

It is certainly a popular hobby and you may start out with serious, long-term intentions in mind. Family history may be particularly attractive to a person approaching retirement as it can be a time-taking activity. If you enjoy travel you may want to coincide your hobby with visits to old churches, villages, old houses, war memorials, and historic county towns where records are often stored. You can usually link your genealogical work with other enjoyable pastimes. It can add a special purpose and some excitement to an otherwise ordinary summer outing. You may want to land a special person or unusual event in your ancestral records – rather like a journalist chases a news coup. Readers already 'into' computers will find plenty of synergy and will tend to major on this side of family history research. Don't just ask the question 'what do I want' once. Ask it from time to time as you experience the very different sides to the subject. Ask it when you seem to get snowed under with 'facts' so that you keep perspective and maintain overall direction.

ONE NAME STUDIES

Another popular area is single or one name studies. You may wish to learn all about your name and its origin and distribution around the world, rather than track down your single ancestral line. This is a potentially social form of the hobby and you may wish to contact many living people. Part of this process will reveal the famous, infamous and bizarre examples of those to whom you may well be related, or at least share a common name. Again, you can do your communicating at a computer terminal or get involved in surname groups, reunions and the like, and the whole social thing. The choice is yours.

John Smith of London

A word here about the name itself. Some are very common and others rare. Thus a Smith world fraternity is not a feasible proposition and would not catch on. However, for most people it is a treat to meet others of the same name if your name is not so common. Thousands of one name groups exist, as well as email lists and newsgroups, even for the most uncommon names. As most contact is now via the internet, one name research can be an inexpensive and fascinating interest. Like genealogy and family history, you can pursue one name studies to any degree you wish. Whatever the name, it is a potentially enormous project for which one life will seem all too short.

The relative popularity of your name will affect tracking your ancestors. A very common name is not the easiest to tackle, as you may meet scores even with the same birth or marriage date, so the chance of mistakes is almost endemic. Having said that, it is perfectly feasible, and just means more care and effort. On the other hand, with a very rare name you may find yourself ploughing through whole records without a single name 'hit', but, conversely, there is a greater chance of that hit relating to your own line. Fortunately, the great majority of names are fine for searching and you take the results as you find them. Bear in mind that a name may be more or less common in a different part of the world. However, within a developed country, such as the UK, mobility has been a factor since the industrial revolution, and – whatever their overall frequency – names are widely spread. A few generations ago a village might comprise a handful of dominant family names, and even today your searching may well reveal a local family hotbed. A particular dominance may survive in a current telephone directory – a key source of data for one name studies.

So your one name study aims may depend on:

♦ the surname you are interested in
♦ the time you are ready to give to the activity
♦ the extent to which you want to socialise
♦ your willingness and ability to travel

and many other factors. Having said that, you can have a *provisional* overall aim. You will learn a lot in the first few weeks and you can make a better decision when you have had a go at the sorts of tasks involved. Like wishing you had chosen somebody else's dessert choice when it is brought to the table, you really just need a taste. But whatever you finish up specialising in, basic rules apply about keeping records, transcription (Chapter 4) and being methodical. At minimum, you will then have something worthwhile to show for your work and to pass on even if you don't keep it up.

GETTING STARTED ONLINE

You can start on the computer straight away if you wish. The above preparatory work may span weeks or months as you plan to visit relatives, get a couple of days off work and so on. By doing different tasks in parallel you will have a variety of things to do and will never get bored. If you are already *au fait* with internet mailing lists and online browsing you will soon find your way around the family history sites and can pick up lots of information at your own pace.

I shall assume that you know your way around the computer to some extent, or that you can get help, in particular in using the world wide web, emails, newsgroups etc. Most readers will have somebody in the near family who can guide them through. Alternatively get them to do some work for you, or plan a session with them on their machine once you have absorbed the basics here. Access to computers also gets easier at libraries, internet cafes, public record offices and other organisations so it necessarily forms a big part of a comprehensive book on the subject.

The two main problems of using the internet concern quantity and quality.

◆ The sheer volume and variety of information out there and the danger of getting bogged down and confused. As in a grocery hypermarket, choice is fine if you know what you want, and that can be the problem in a whole new area such as genealogy.
◆ The quality or reliability of the information. With a few exceptions information freely downloadable is liable to be wrong, incomplete, misleading or plain fictitious.

Without exception you need to verify the *sources* of data you find and anything you download. Just remember that the information can be of no better quality than the data an army of unpaid enthusiasts, in the main, laboriously keyed in. Garbage in, garbage out. And very old manuscripts can look positively hieroglyphic (see Chapter 7 on old records), so genealogy has its own special problems of transcription, even with care and attention (see Chapter 4). To ameliorate the pitfalls, try to get into the habit of recording the immediate sources of any information you print out or download – the website, newsgroup or whatever. That information, such as from the IGI, will usually have cited sources in turn (such as a parish register), which is one of the things you will have to get used to.

In practice, you should be able to limit main record searches of baptisms, marriages and burials to a few websites and work in a fairly standardised way. Additional information you discover in due course will tend to be, in its nature, textual, such as anecdotes and explanations, and more subjective than even old parish register transcriptions. Once you stray from the main sources, such as public civil records of births and marriage registration, the risk of error and unreliable sources multiplies. At least by stating your sources your successors can judge for themselves how credible they are and you will not be cursed posthumously out of hand.

Cyberspace savvy

As well as doing a few name searches, as you explore each website, you will learn about family history generally, the range of records available and where they are located, and the inside world of this growing interest. There are literally thousands of genealogy-related sites on the world wide web, hence our identifying the top sites (Chapter 2) and including the guidelines in FH internet resources generally (Chapter 3). Many of these websites are run by suppliers and service providers, such as software sellers, professional genealogists and freelance researchers. Many started as mutual help support for enthusiasts and continue to be so except that once they become successful (by number of 'visits') they can attract advertisers and so raise revenue.

Almost nothing on the internet is without some axe to grind, and if there is such a site it is advisable to accept the caveat. This is particularly important in terms of the reliability or authenticity of what you may wish to draw from a web site. Thankfully, there are professional organisations, such as the Society of Genealogists and the Federation of Family History Societies, and these not-for-profit organisations are replete with useful information for novices and experts alike. Similarly, the main record offices now have their own web sites, such as the Family Records Centre and the Public Records Office in London. The BBC also has an excellent family history section on its main site.

Be sure to differentiate between original material prepared by an organisation, such as printable leaflets, online guides and articles by members, and the many links to which their site may take you, over which they have no control, of course. Cyndi's List website (featured in detail in Chapter 3), although of extraordinary size and wealth of content, is in reality more of a clearing house or family history directory. Used as such, this and similar sites are valuable resources. More specialised family history related organisations are increasingly getting a presence on the internet but for a while the presentation and usability standards may not compete with the big ones.

Finally there are hundreds of thousands of individual sites on which individuals and families post their own family histories. These are often linked, in various ways such as through family history society and single name websites, and share each others' information. They range from small family sites with photographs of the dogs and Clara's school report to large GEDCOM (Chapter 2) repositories that you may hit upon on your own online journeys.

Doing a name search

You can make a start by keying in your surname on a few internet sites to see what comes up. Far better if you have a first name as well, say of a great, great grandparent, and a date or approximate date of birth. The earlier the date, the greater your chance of a 'hit', as online indices tend to become sparse at the beginning of the twentieth century – not 'real' genealogy to some people. Try the following sites for starters, covered in much more detail in Chapter 2.

familysearch.com
ancestry.com

Treat this initial search as an interesting start on the internet in parallel with the more important work of finding all you can from within your family. Get familiar with finding your way around these sites, what they contain, and in particular where your own name seems to get responses. If you come across a person who seems to 'fit' make a copy of the page, or download it onto a main disk folder set up for the purpose, and which you can refer to at any time. If you are not ready to search online, Chapter 2 gives a fuller preview of what screen inputs look like, and the sort of genealogy reports you can print out.

START UP GUIDELINES

The following rules, tips, principles and guidelines will help towards a painless start, whatever approach you want to take to family history. More important, they will provide the right foundation for a pleasurable, long-term interest in the subject that will more than reward your time and effort.

♦ Work backwards. You may well have a famous ancestor but you can never be sure until you have made the connection in a 'tree' that connects to your mum or dad. Add a 'great' to your great-grandparent and one more 'great' at a time. The more recent the records are, the more reliable and legible they will tend to be. You will therefore meet the joys of funny spelling and handwriting *gradually* as you work further back in time. This experience is a natural sort of training so you will not need to attend Old English or palaeography classes unless and until you decide to specialise in such a way. Censuses may break the 'work backwards' rule. In this case you can search the earliest census *after* a firm birth or marriage date, thus verifying your name and date information and adding more, such as the exact address of your ancestors. Going forward to the next centennial census you will reconfirm the growing siblings and omissions for marriage, death or whatever, or draw a blank if the family have moved out of the house or census district. However, it makes sense to establish a firm lineage working backwards before you start to expand information from censuses working in the opposite time direction.

♦ Have a method. Any method is better than none when it comes to keeping records. Just bear in mind that ancestry records grow like Topsy, like twigs and leaves on a tree as compared with its single trunk and few main branches, so you will need spare capacity in every part of your recording system. Make these common sense principles more than good ideas, but part of your routine way of tracking, recording and filing information. If you need help, you can get ABC record-keeping guidelines on some of the main FH websites we cover in the book.

♦ Do as much as you can before you arrive at a record office, such as preparing separate sheets for different records or types of records. This not only fulfils the previous 'method' requirement, but you will save valuable time you can spend instead on actual transcription during your limited time with the source documents. You will find more about specific preparation in Chapter 6 covering public records and Chapter 7 that addresses old records.

♦ Don't rely on your memory, even if you have a good one. An abbreviation that seems obvious at the time when hurrying to complete some notes before closing time at a record office can appear as rural mandarin not many months later. Even worse, after making no record because you found nothing of use, you may find yourself trawling the same source a year on, forgetting that you had already drawn a blank. Like good detective work, eliminating people and factors is as important as adding 'suspects'. Get into the habit of recording, not just what you *find,* but what, where and when you *look* for anything. A large day-to-a-page diary is a handy record as it can accommodate all this as well as being a genealogy diary of times and places you visit.

◆ When at the record office follow a system that will economise on your time. For example, plan to get all the information you need out of a record rather than refer to it one particular name at a time. This means planning before you leave home, of course. You can also save time in the way you marshal your data to input to a software program, which will usually favour doing a whole person or family record at a time. In short, think ahead.

◆ Transcribe data exactly as you find it. This rule applies also to layout, such as the order of columns of a census form. You will soon become familiar with layouts of registers and certificates, so a different, personal layout will be confusing later. Transcribe errors and all. You will soon get used to abbreviations and spelling differences and this will become a routine part of your research. Don't correct 'obvious' mistakes, at least at the hands-on transcribing stage. Don't make quick judgements about relationships – the 'thinking' work can come later. Chapter 4 covers transcription in more detail.

◆ In particular, keep to spellings you find, and, as a general rule, do not abbreviate. The exception is standardised abbreviations for phrases such as 'in memory of' or 'lawful son of' where there can be no misunderstanding. In this case the rule reverses, and you write out anything in full that is *not* a standard phrase. A single word can make all the difference. For example, in Scotland 'of' a place means owner, whereas 'in' refers to an inhabitant. You can also abbreviate a field that recurs over whole batches of documents such as the parish name (more of this in Chapter 7).

◆ Do not expand name abbreviations you find in original documents. An abbreviation such as Jos. can refer to more than one name. These will become clear as you get more data and corroborate it by relationships. More about abbreviations in Chapter 7.

◆ Indicate omissions from an original with the convention '. . .'. If you are not sure about an interpretation, show this by '[(?)]'. If you add an alternative interpretation show this as '[=?]'. If you add anything, put it in square brackets.

◆ Copy an original record or letter exactly as it appears. You may make more sense of it as your experience, of both palaeography and name abbreviation, grows. After hours of work at a record office it may be tempting to write what you would *like* the word to be. Don't be tempted – just copy what you find.

◆ Make your notes the *only* notes from the original – don't resolve to write them out neatly later. That just adds another transcription stage and a further source of error (if your resolution is ever fulfilled). Necessary copying, such as to a chart or other record back at home, needs to be as careful as if you were copying from the original. That makes legibility of the your 'original' notes that much more important.

◆ Make notes of names and dates of interest even if they do not seem directly relevant at the time. They may prove to be an important link later, and you need to get as much potential value as possible from what may be one shot only at the originals, or a time-taking trip to a record office.

◆ Make a record of what you have copied and what you have not. For example, all examples of a certain name or just some? And on what basis did you pick and choose? Did you do a scrupulous word for word check or did you scan the document in a hurry? This simple information will be worth its weight in leather bound indices if and when you make a return visit.

◆ Make a note of any gaps in your research, such as a period of dates, or a record you did not get hold of, or if you left off a task partway through. You may need to do another trip to a record source later anyway, so you need to know exactly where you left off and what, for any reason, you missed. One big mistake of this sort, that can take many hours to rectify, is probably all you need to never do it again. But even one mistake is easily avoidable if you follow simple rules.

◆ Always record the reference of any source if there is one – such as volume and page or folio numbers, as well as the record office. This is what gives validity to your research and adds professionalism. It also makes life easier if and when you want to obtain a copy of the original.

◆ Record the dates and places of your research. Information such as this can be in a diary, either a special family history diary for the purpose, or a regular personal or business diary.

◆ Have a friend who has the same interest. Join the local family history society – most larger towns have one. It doesn't matter that your family hails from the other end of the country, you can pick up lots of free information and advice. A knowledgeable friend at your 'target' location is equally useful, as they may accompany you to the local record office. You can establish contact quickly by telephone, email and correspondence once you are a member of a society or subscribe to a mailing list (see Chapter 3). You will also meet some addicts and bores, of course, but that is a danger in any absorbing activity and you will have to trust your innate level-headedness.

◆ Don't go off at tangents. Old records can be so intriguing that you are tempted to pursue anything of interest, even if it is not part of your family history aims. This is not to deny pleasure in the hobby. You have as much chance of exploring interesting clues and ideas that are of potential value to your stated aims as from other material you happen to come across. You will realise that the need for self discipline crops up in many aspects of family history research. The same principle applied to restricting your overall aims – say to a single family line – but we are usually more vulnerable to instinctual and irrational behaviour in the heady atmosphere of hands-on research than when writing up a master plan. Suddenly the afternoon is gone and you realise you haven't got half of what you set out to get. Stay focused.

2

Online Family Searching

This chapter introduces in more detail the two websites I referred to in the last chapter – **familysearch.com** and **ancestry.com.** If you are not familiar with internet searching generally this will explain online family searching step by step. If you are new to family history it will explain the kind of information you can find, and the part the world wide web can play especially in basic genealogy based on vital public records. What you learn will be of particular value when you get back a few centuries in the records, when spelling and other conventions differ a lot from today. It will also help you to get your family name ancestry right, given the possible pitfalls, as this is what your family history will build upon. First, I have included a section on surnames as these will be your focus for a while and a little background knowledge may make your early endeavours go smoother and create more interest.

SURNAMES

You may want to use surnames in one of two main ways. One name studies are popular, and these relate to a single surname usually on a worldwide or countrywide basis, regardless of individual family lines. If your name is uncommon, this can be an interesting kind of research and a fascinating hobby in its own right. The other use of surnames is in the course of genealogy and family history research when the surname is your prime focus of interest. This may be a single paternal or maternal name tracked as far back as you can, or one or more of the many names you can trace by following marriage lines.

Many family historians have an interest in all these aspects of surnames. It may depend on how common or uncommon your family name is, a special purpose for the study (like verifying a family legend), or what most appeals to you as a hobby. You may wish to do a single name study as a one-off project, but take up family history as an ongoing project. At the same time, whilst your main aim may be to trace your own surname as a single blood line as far back as possible – perhaps collecting as much additional information as possible after BDMs – you may have reason to stray along specific marriage lines for particular purposes. Maybe somebody famous lies along that tree, or a daughter emigrated, giving an interesting new line of investigation and so on. Or you may acquire a whole chunk of ancestry along a branch in the course of your research without having to do any hard work.

You can establish the presence of a surname on the internet easily by referring to the RootsWeb Surname List, part of the main rootsweb.com site. You can also try the Guild of One Name Studies we cover in Chapter 5. Just as easily, you can search the two main websites we cover in this chapter. A multi-browser search engine such as Copernic (you can download this software free) will also produce a formidable response unless your surname is extremely uncommon.

It is as well to establish the approximate scale of internet presence of your family name quite early. This may influence your decisions about where to focus your research and will give important information about what has already been done. Whilst there is nothing wrong with doing your own original research from scratch, you may decide that if you can obtain readymade ancestral relationships you may as well put your effort into other aspects of research. For example, you can study a particular date period, or branches of the tree that have not been covered, or find more information about the people and how they lived, or you could specialise in your own geographical area and contribute to a one name study.

You have a good chance of tracing back a surname to a time when most people could not write, let alone spell correctly. The educated – or at least basically literate – people who recorded names, such as parish clerks, relied on the sounds of names and were not too scrupulous about getting a phonetic match, let alone consistency from person to person with the same sounding name. In fact the very concept of a correct spelling would have been unknown. So, not only will you probably find any number of variants, but further back the name may have been so corrupted that further tracking is impractical. This is the sort of background information we will cover before starting on web searches.

Hereditary names

Surnames, or family names passed on from generation to generation, are a recent innovation in the context of recorded history. Even among the nobility who wanted to preserve their heritage, names only started to pass from father to son in about the early 12th century. In the following century they spread gradually among the common people but most people did not possess a hereditary surname until about the end of the 14th century. However, at the point most searches for family names effectively start – that is, at the time when parish registers were introduced in 1538 (in England) – hereditary names (spelling notwithstanding) were quite universal in England, and later in Scotland.

Origins

The origin of hereditary names as such was because of the need to identify people for administrative and fiscal purposes, but the origin of individual surnames is far more fascinating and deserves a study in its own right. The name related to the person in some logical way to practically identify him among his neighbours. For example, it might be the name the father was known as, such as George, or Robert/s. There are scores of 'first name' surnames that remain today. Others known by the place they were associated with, especially those from outside the locality, such as York, London or Chester, or even a nearby village. Other names referred to a craft or occupation, which were usually passed from father to son anyway, such as Carpenter, Miller, Cowper and Farmer. Nicknames, or descriptive names were also common, and these related to some physical feature or temperamental characteristic of the person just as they do today. We can only guess at the diverse origins of these names other than the obvious Littles and Biggs.

Initially these additional names were not hereditary but might change from time to time throughout a person's life such as when starting an apprenticeship, moving to another locality or even at the whim of some literate clerk making a record. The person in any event might use a different name from the one that happened to be used in some official record.

The process of hereditary names came later in Scotland and Ireland, and later still in Wales, in which stable surnames did not appear until the 18th century and even later. All this affects genealogy, as do a myriad aspects of the historical times your ancestry will span. Bringing local and national history to life, rather than just the individual 'roots' aspect, is part of the fascination of the subject. There are plenty of books on the origins of surnames if you want to specialise, or just to get more information about the particular surnames your research uncovers.

One name studies

You will probably find it interesting to check on the distribution of your surname today, and telephone directories are an easy source. Some people do this intuitively when visiting another country. However, any distribution will have changed over the centuries with the mass migration during the industrial revolution, the general rural to urban movement and new world emigration. Nevertheless, there are still hotbeds of particular surnames that date back as far as the parish records. You can get a lot of information about the distribution of names in the 18th century from Bardsley's dictionary (A dictionary of English and Welsh surnames, C W Bardsley) that any main reference library should have. Or you will find introductory information on the Society of Genealogists website. The Journal of One Names Studies features research in this area of genealogy, and a short visit to the Guild of One Name Studies (GOONS) website (covered in Chapter 5) will get you started.

Many indexes list names under a standard spelling (such as Soundex, used in the IGI) and this makes searching very much easier. There are risks, of course, but you will need to verify what you find by relationships and other corroboration rather than a particular spelling and date in any case. Bear in mind that anybody can change their name if they wish to, and you don't even need to record it – although this is more of a nuisance nowadays with credit cards, benefits and suchlike. Name changes that have been recorded such as by deed poll are searchable just like other names. The Society of Genealogists suggests reference sources if you reach this stage in your research.

Surnames on the internet

As well as those already mentioned, surname resources are at soc.genealogy.surnames.britain and soc.genealogysurnames .ireland. GenServ is a volunteer-operated collection of family history GEDCOM files, from which you can have a trial 60-day access if you submit your own files – a mutual, or reciprocal resource. Rootsweb comprises a community of thousands of web pages where you can search for names. There are links to information on getting started, family history centres, the ROOTS-L mailing lists and genealogy-related files you can request by email and lots more. For example an article entitled Computers: Changing the Face of Genealogy (relatively old [1989] but valid). Surname Helper lets you search for a surname linking you to its website source anywhere in the world, such as a UK county GenWeb project. The World GenWeb project is a non-profit, volunteer based project collecting genealogical data around the world. FreeREG provides details of baptisms, marriages and burial records. It is part of the FreeUKGEN project and companion to FreeBDM. These are just being developed at the time of writing. You can also browse or search for surnames on ancestralfindings.com, where you will get email addresses of the people doing the research.

The RSL, or RootsWeb surnames list is a fast-growing registry of over a million surnames submitted by genealogists around the world. Like ancestralfindings.com it gives information about the person submitting the name, so – at least for the more uncommon names – can be a source of specific help in your research. If your surname is not on the list you can add it and it may attract new contributions. If too many results are thrown up you may need to narrow your search with given names and dates as we shall see with the two websites we will now address.

The Society of Genealogists have a search facility of articles that have featured surnames in the Genealogist's Magazine. The volume is considerably greater than published biographies so many readers will get hits. The writers of the articles may be useful contacts.

FAMILYSEARCH.COM

FamilySearch.com is the website of the Church of Jesus Christ of Latter-Day Saints, or Mormons. The church holds massive databases centrally at Salt Lake City, Utah, and many of these can be accessed at local Family History Centres around the world. These are generally open to the public and searchable at no cost and you may have a centre within reach – you can find the locations on this website.

Although biased to the needs of church members, the site offers lots of helpful information on tracing your ancestors, which you can use as you wish. In fact you may at first find the site too big and detailed, as it serves very dedicated researchers as well as church members and the general public.

Doing a name search

On entering the site, you can make a start searching with the name and approximate birth date of your earliest known ancestor from the Getting Started chapter. Choose 'all records' which includes the IGI index plus the Pedigree Resource File and the Ancestral File (see below). Initially, in addition to first and last name, specify just the country (England, Ireland, Scotland, or Wales as the case may be) and a date, which can be approximate within a specified range of years. The process is simple and you can refine a search if the number of hits is unmanageable (depending on how common or rare a name is), and if you have more information such as a place or more precise date. Otherwise just plough through the list. Overleaf is the main on-screen search form which is typical of online name searches.

Events in the drop down menu include births/baptisms, marriages and deaths/burials. You can choose to approximate the date to plus or minus 2, 5, 10 or 20 years. So, given a fairly uncommon name, you can search through the generations quite quickly in 40 year (+ or – 20 years) jumps.

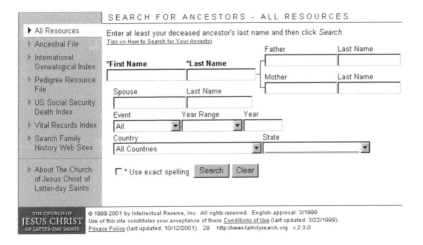

FIGURE 1 FamilySearch input.

You can opt for the search to cover all records held ('all records'), which includes the IGI already referred to, and also databases of family trees already created, submitted and consolidated in the site. Individual search results can be downloaded as pages, printed off, or downloaded as GEDCOM files.

GEDCOM

The LDS has done a lot to standardise genealogical recording and pioneered the GEDCOM standard for transferring genealogical information from computer to computer around the world. This makes it easy to share family information, and in particular enforces a common standard of content and terminology. You can add GEDCOM files to your own family history program individually or in large chunks, to immediately enlarge your ancestry tree. Most family history software programs allow you to import and export GEDCOM files so you don't need to understand them technically to make use of them.

When doing a name search remember that FamilySearch will not search for a first name only, and it ignores middle names unless you tick the 'exact spelling' box. In that case the search will be for the first, middle and last name exactly as you key them in. That is fine if you are sure about a spelling, or you know a record is in the database and you want to get straight to it without poring over long lists of name variants. Otherwise it is safer to use the default Soundex system (don't tick anything) that captures all similar sounding versions of the name. If you tick 'exact spelling' you may not input parents, spouse, event, year or country.

You can search for just a last name, but no more than 25 results will be shown from each source. You can then request up to 200 results from a source. So for common surnames you will need to fill in additional fields to make your search more manageable. This is where your initial investigations among the family will prove to be valuable, even if just an approximate date. A surname only search will indicate the volume of entries you are dealing with so you can decide how to proceed.

International Genealogical Index (IGI)
FamilySearch's very large searchable databases include the International Genealogical Index (IGI) which includes basic

information on baptisms and marriages largely drawn from parish registers. This is an index so should not be treated as a primary or even secondary source. It lets you know whether the record you are searching is included in the database and if so its primary source and reference.

The index is far from complete and at the same time there is lots of duplication. A 'person' may appear dozens of times because of tiny variances in the content of the record fields, such as name spellings, date approximations and the absence or presence of a spouse, parents, place of birth and suchlike. At the same time there are doubts about the authenticity of many of the early submissions of church members, and even more so about entries from the wider public. However, because of its sheer size, it is an obvious early port of call as an index.

The site, understandably, is biased towards an American audience. However, the United Kingdom and Ireland are a prime focus for millions of Americans tracing their roots and a lot of the information they contribute is as valid and useful as data you can obtain on some of the big UK sites. LDS market their own family history software for keeping your computer records and producing charts and reports. It also sells CD ROMS with various searchable databases – again mainly US directed. You can find details on the website, or you can do a full web search of 'genealogy software' to get reviews and user sites as well as vendors. Amazon.co.uk also sell a range of FH software.

You will find that twentieth century IGI records are sparser than the nineteenth, so they may not give hits for the first couple of 'great greats' you search. If the person you want to trace was born in your present county locality, so much the better, as you can do a search at your local public record office. Otherwise initial online searching can save a lot of time and you can travel to the record office from whence your ancestors come, armed with specific enquiries. An IGI search for an individual for whom you have an approximate birth year may provide the names and birth/baptism dates of father and mother, from which you can work successively back in time. The inclusion of a spouse's name may help to confirm the identity of a person. As I have already said, treat these results with caution until you can corroborate them by fuller family relationships and in due course from actual copies of birth certificates, which we cover later.

Overleaf is an individual printout from a name search. Notice that no parents are shown, and this is to be expected as parish registers did not start until 1538 and were decidedly iffy for quite some years. Christening or infant baptism, rather than birth date, is usually cited where records are parish registers. In other records you will come across, a baptism date may be shown as b bef (born before). Although approximated (sometimes several years separate the two dates), this allows births to be consolidated with later actual birth dates from civil births, deaths and marriages certificates.

Although not specific to this site, we can pick up some background information from these records. The middle name 'Aldren' was probably the way the family name was spelt by the parish priest or clerk on hearing it pronounced by a proud but illiterate parent. The actual spelling variant is often included in brackets after the modern version of the

John Aldren ALDER

　Sex: M

Event(s):

　Birth: 1555

　　　Kings Stanley, Gloucester, England

Parents:

Source Information:

　Film Number:　6142787

　Page Number:

　Reference Number:

FIGURE 2　FamilySearch IGI output

family name (John (Aldren) Alder). Lots of spellings appear for some surnames – and indeed for 'given' or Christian names – and the appropriately named Soundex system collects all these similar sounding names when you do a search. This is an invaluable resource when you get back to the sixteenth and seventeenth centuries in particular, before common spelling and indeed literacy. The Soundex system will pick up all the phonetic variants of a name, but also allows you the odd mistyping when you enter a name.

Ancestral File

As well as the IGI, which comprises individual records (perhaps with parents and spouse), the Ancestral File can be searched, and is included in 'all records'. This database shows several generations of people and how they are related. These comprise pedigrees and family group sheets, and identify the person who submitted them. Individual Ancestral File records (not pedigree trees) can be downloaded.

Pedigree Resource File

The Pedigree Resource File is a lineage-linked (different family trees joined up as bigger, connecting trees) database of records submitted by individuals through Family Search Internet. There is a version accessible free on the internet, and another, with more detail, available on CD ROM. The internet version does not include text notes accompanying basic data, nor detail about sources, but it does give reference numbers enabling you to search the CD ROM which has all the database information. Anybody can print or download individual records from this website database. From the CD ROM, which you can buy direct from the site and (convenient for British people) at most Family History Centres and the SoG, you can also print charts and reports, as well as notes and detailed sources.

The LDS have developed their own family history software, Personal Ancestral File and a basic version of this can be downloaded free from the site.

Family History Centres

On the site you can find details of Family History Centres around the world. There are some 3,700 centres in 88 countries so there is a good chance there is one in a large town near you. You can check by doing a 'place' search – I located the Liverpool centre in about 20 seconds. Note that the centres cannot handle mail enquiries, and nor can they do searches for you if you visit, although you will find the staff helpful regarding the records held and how to read them.

Family Search Library

The LDS has an enormous genealogical library at the Salt Lake City headquarters and you can also search this, under the 'Catalogue' tab, by name, place, author, subject, and record reference. Entering an English parish name, for example, will probably confirm that transcriptions of the parish and census records are held in the library.

Under the 'Library' menu you will find an 'Education' tab, and here you can find first rate guidance about research. This is classified by place, and includes England, Ireland, Scotland and Wales, further subdivided into the periods from 1066 to the start of parish registers in 1538, the period 1538 to 1837 when civil B, D and M registration was introduced, and from 1837 to the present date. Detailed instruction leaflets are downloadable in PDF format (the software is free to download from this site), including how to search for birth, death, marriage and census records, and places throughout the United Kingdom. The Education Services also include publications, including forms to help record making, home study courses, and information on conferences and genealogical institutions. Give yourself plenty of time to explore this site – it's a gold-mine. Be ready to copy, download or 'bookmark' useful guidance and reference material as you meet it to save retracing your steps at a later date.

ANCESTRY.COM

This popular site holds another huge set of databases. Much of the site can be searched without a charge, in particular 'vital' data on births, marriages and deaths. The advantage over the FamilySearch site is that you can print or download whole ancestry (back) or pedigree (forwards from an ancestor) trees, being ready-made hierarchies of relationships that others have contributed. A single search with a date may provide the direct ancestral tree as far back as the data included on the site. As with the IGI, you can download this information as GEDCOM files and incorporate it into any popular family history software program (don't buy one that does not handle GEDCOM files). Like the IGI, whether you find some of your own family tree depends on what has been submitted to the site by others. It is far from a complete index so some readers may draw a blank on their name searches.

You can print out a family tree either as charts or text relationship hierarchies. If you strike lucky with your particular name you might produce a direct line back to the seventeenth or sixteenth century in an hour or so. This is where the computer comes into its own, as such a feat might take days or weeks of searching at record offices. The information in ancestry.com has been transcribed from civil public records and parish registers so will have a reasonable chance of accuracy. As with familysearch.com, spellings need not be critical as these databases use the Soundex system. However, as I repeat throughout the book, only by reference to original records (such as birth and marriage certificates and parish registers of christening, marriage and burial), can you be sure of the validity of an online record.

The records also contain notes made by the various compilers and this can lead you to more information about a person such as has been obtained from a will, military service record, letters and so on. Once again, you should refer back to the original source for reliable information. The source document reference is part of the data required for submission to this and similar sites so that you and I will be spared effort at least in tracking down where the data purports to come from.

The on screen search form is similar to the one on the previous LDS search site.

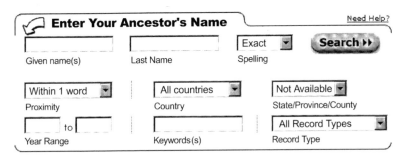

FIGURE 3   ancestry.com name search input

The same search at the LDS site produces a more useful result at ancestry.com. The main advantage is the scope of information regarding person-to-person relationships, and the ready-made linkage into descendency and pedigree hierarchies.

Robin's Ancestors

Entries: 1331   **Updated:** Sat Aug 25 17:57:00 2001
Contact: robin roberts <robin_f_roberts@email.msn.com>

Index / Descendency / Register / Download GEDCOM / Add Post-em

☐ *ID:* I48126627
☐ *Name:* John (Aldren) ALDER
☐ *Given Name:* John (Aldren)
☐ *Surname:* ALDER
☐ *Sex:* M
☐ *Birth:* Bef 1557
☐ *Death:* Aft 1617
☐ *Religion:* RR9216
☐ *Change Date:* 19 Nov 1996
☐ *Note:* HIST: @NI043@

Marriage 1 Susan SIMS b: Bef 1557

　　　　• *Married:* 25 Oct 1571 in Standish, Gls

Children

　　　1.　Elizabeth ALDER b: Abt 1572 in Kings Stanley, Gls
　　　2.　Elizabeth ALDER
　　　3.　Elizabeth ALDER
　　　4.　Catherine ALDER
　　　5.　Toby ALDER
　　　6.　Suzana ALDER
　　　7.　Toby ALDER
　　　8.　John (Alderne) ALDER b: Bef 1589
　　　9.　Margery (Aldren) ALDER
　　10.　Alice (Aldren) ALDER
　　11.　Ellioner (Aldren) ALDER

Sources:

1. Text: Latest year calculated from established date of marriage

FIGURE 4　　ancestry.com name search output

There is a lot more information than the same familysearch.com result, as the spouse and children are shown. Similar information for each of the children can be got with a hyperlink click, and in the case of this example the various lines can be tracked forward right into the twentieth century.

From the heading you will note that 'Robin' has produced this particular batch of data. This is useful information as you can contact Robin directly with questions. As you move to and fro through the generations it may switch to a different contributor but the hyperlinks are maintained. The head icon against child number 8 indicates that the person has children (or, more precisely, that the database contains records of children), so a link to those children will expand the information to include a possible spouse and more children.

Figure 5 shows a portion of the descendency tree you can print or download in text format.

Notice all the variants of the spelling shown in brackets. This retains a better link to the original document, warts and all, although it occurs less and less as you move towards the later centuries.

You can also select a pedigree chart showing the ancestral tree. John (Aldren) Alder (No 1), born in about 1555, is the oldest IGI entry so he doesn't have any ancestry to display. If you choose John (Alday) (6) the first son of Samuel (Alderne) d aft 1717 (5) – or anyone in the tree of descendants of John (Aldren) 1555 – you can print out a

1 <u>John (Aldren) ALDER</u> b: Bef 1557 d: Aft 1617
+ <u>Susan SIMS</u> b: Bef 1557 d: Aft 1591
  2 <u>Elizabeth ALDER</u> b: Abt 1572
  2 <u>Elizabeth ALDER</u> d: Bef 1576
  2 <u>Elizabeth ALDER</u> d: Bef 1617
  2 <u>Catherine ALDER</u> d: Aft 1617
  2 <u>Toby ALDER</u> d: Bef 1584
  2 <u>Suzana ALDER</u> d: Aft 1671
  2 <u>Toby ALDER</u> d: Aft 1671
  2 <u>John (Alderne) ALDER</u> b: Bef 1589
    3 <u>Josias (Alderne) ALDER</u>
    3 <u>John (Aldaye) ALDER</u> d: Aft 1655
      4 <u>Mary (Allderne) ALDER</u> d: Bef 1649
      4 <u>John (Alderne) ALDER</u> d: Aft 1669
      4 <u>Josaias (Alderne) ALDER</u> d: Aft 1667
        + <u>Margrey (Strittford) STRATFORD</u> d: Abt 1677
      5 <u>Jeremy (Alderne) ALDER</u>
      5 <u>Josias (Alderne) ALDER</u> d: Bef 1681
      5 <u>Samuel (Alderne) ALDER</u> d: Aft 1717
        6 <u>John (Alday) ALDER</u>
        6 <u>Samuel (Alday) ALDER</u>
        6 <u>Gyles (Alday) ALDER</u>
        6 <u>Thomas (Alday) ALDER</u> d: Aft 1734
        6 <u>Daniel (Alday) ALDER</u>
          + <u>Sarah TROTMAN</u>
        6 <u>Mary (Alday) ALDER</u> d: Bef 1717
        6 <u>Susanah (Alday) ALDER</u>
        6 <u>Elizabeth (Alday) ALDER</u>
        6 <u>Sarah (Alday) ALDER</u>
        6 <u>Nathaniel (Alday) ALDER</u> d: Aft 1745
        6 <u>Benjamin (Alday) ALDER</u>
        6 <u>Timothy (Alday) ALDER</u> d: Aft 1756
        6 <u>Martha (Alday) ALDER</u>
        6 <u>Mary (Alday) ALDER</u>
      5 <u>Mary (Alday) ALDER</u> d: Aft 1707
        + <u>Jone LEVETT</u>
      5 <u>Josyah (Alday) ALDER</u>
      5 <u>Richard (Alday) ALDER</u>
      5 <u>John (Alday) ALDER</u> d: Bef 1702
      5 <u>John (Alday) ALDER</u>
      5 <u>Josyah (Alday) ALDER</u> d: Bef 1688
    4 <u>Mary (Alderne) ALDER</u>
    4 <u>William (Alday) ALDER</u> d: aft 19 Feb 1722/1723
    3 <u>Sisley (Aldrne) ALDER</u>
    3 <u>Jeremy (Alderne) ALDER</u>
    3 <u>Elizabeth (Alderne) ALDER</u>
  2 <u>Margery (Aldren) ALDER</u> d: Aft 1615
  2 <u>Alice (Aldren) ALDER</u> d: Bef 1617
  2 <u>Ellioner (Aldren) ALDER</u> d: Aft 1617

FIGURE 5 ancestry.com Descendency Tree output

chart of ancestors. Figure 6 is the simple text version of the pedigree of John, son of Samuel. (He [John] didn't seem to have a wife [or one that managed to reach the IGI]).

```
                                /John (Aldren) ALDER b: Bef 1557 d: Aft 1617
                    /John (Alderne) ALDER b: Bef 1589
                    |           \Susan SIMS b: Bef 1557 d: Aft 1591
              /John (Aldaye) ALDER d: Aft 1655
         /Josaias (Alderne) ALDER d: Aft 1667
  /Samuel (Alderne) ALDER d: Aft 1717
  |       |                   /Roger (Streatford) STRATFORD b: Abt 1550 d:
  |       |         /Thomas (Statforde) STRATFORD d: Aft 1618
  |       |      /Thomas (Stretford) STRATFORD d: Aft 1636
  |       \Margrey (Strittford) STRATFORD d: Abt 1677
John (Alday) ALDER
```

FIGURE 6   ancestry.com Pedigree Chart

This presentation as printed out is a bit scrappy. You can also select a conventional tree, or cascade diagram but this is far too big to fit on a page. The other form of presentation you can choose is ahnentafel (below). As an example I have chosen Josias (3 on descendency tree on p. 52), son of John and Margery (2).

The ahnentafel system

The generation numbers 1 to 3 follow what is known as the ahnentafel system of genealogical numbering (see Figure 7). This is a German word meaning 'ancestor table' and the system is used universally by genealogists. The starting person is number 1, their father is number 2 and their mother is number 3. The father's father is number 4 and his mother number 5. The mother's father is 6 and the mother's mother is 7. Any individual's father is his or her number multiplied by 2. Except for number 1, all males have even numbers and females have odd numbers. It can be shown as a simple chart (forget the numbers in the descendency chart – the numbers

Ahnentafel, Generation No. 1

1. **Josias (Alderne) ALDER**. He was the son of 2. **John (Alderne) ALDER.**

Ahnentafel, Generation No. 2

2. **John (Alderne) ALDER** was born Bef 1589. He was the son of 4. **John (Aldren) ALDER** and 5. **Susan SIMS**.

Children of John (Aldeme) ALDER are:

1.　i. Josias (Alderne) ALDER.
　　ii. John (Aldaye) ALDER died Aft 1655.
　　iii. Sisley (Aldrne) ALDER.
　　iv. Jeremy (Alderne) ALDER.
　　v. Elizabeth (Alderne) ALDER.

Ahnentafel, Generation No. 3

4. **John (Aldren) ALDER** was born Bef 1557, and died Aft 1617.
5. **Susan SIMS** was born Bef 1557, and died Aft 1591.

Children of Susan SIMS and John (Aldren) ALDER are:

　　i. Elizabeth ALDER was born Abt 1572 in Kings Stanley, G1s.
　　ii. Elizabeth ALDER died Bef 1576.
　　iii. Elizabeth ALDER died Bef 1617.
　　iv. Catherine ALDER died Aft 1617.
　　v. Toby ALDER died Bef 1584 in Kings Stanley, G1s.
　　vi. Suzana ALDER died Aft 1671.
　　vii Toby ALDER died Aft 1671 in Kings Stanley, GIs.
2.　viii. John (Alderne) ALDER was born Bef 1589.
　　ix. Margery (Aldren) ALDER died Aft 1615.
　　x. Alice (Aldren) ALDER died Bef 1617.
　　xi. Ellioner (Aldren) ALDER died Aft 1617.

FIGURE 7　ancestry.com ahnentafel output

here have a special meaning). Imagine you are Fred, or insert your own name.

Generation	Number	Relationship
1	1	Fred
2	2	Fred's father
	3	Fred's mother
3	4	Fred's father's father
	5	Fred's father's mother
	6	Fred's mother's father
	7	Fred's mother's mother
4	8	Fred's father's father's father
	9	Fred's father's father's mother
	10	Fred's father's mother's father
	11	Fred's father's mother's mother
	12	Fred's mother's father's father
	13	Fred's mother's father's mother
	14	Fred's mother's mother's father

With each successive generation the number of ancestors doubles. You will need to get familiar with the different presentations of family trees, especially when swapping records with other researchers.

Other ancestry.com resources

All the earlier charts were printed out free of charge from the website and as you see you can choose different layout formats. Alternatively you can download GEDCOM files into your own or proprietary FH software and print it out in one of the formats the software supports, or merge it into your own database to produce an expanded family tree.

Important datasets on the ancestry.com site are restricted to members who pay a charge. These include Pallot's Marriage

Index and parish register transcripts. The complete ancestry.com database can be viewed free of charge at the SoG library.

As well as being useful for initial searches, this site, like familysearch.com, has helpful information and advice that you can download, so you may wish to spend a bit of time exploring it. Under the 'Learn' tab, then 'Library', then 'Browse the Library' tab you can access literally thousands of items posted mostly by individuals on every aspect of genealogy. These are heavily US biased but there are enough relating to England, Ireland, Scotland and Wales to make a browse worthwhile. For example, the headings cover:

- How To
- record sources
- family origins
- technology
- organisations
- geography
- preserving family history
- home sources
- religion
- genealogy products
- current events
- historical context

– too much to even begin to describe.

I will give two examples I found helpful out of scores directly relating to British genealogy. These were under the 'Historical Context' link. First, an article about the actual journey to the

USA that thousands of British people underwent from their home parish that may have been many miles from the embarkation port, to their final US destination many months later. Second, an article about immigrants into Britain in well-researched European 'waves' from the earliest records. These make interesting reading and may stimulate further research.

If any topic headings are of interest to you when you visit this or any site you may as well print out or download the article rather than risk forgetting where you had seen it. Another good discipline is to organise folders and subfolders to hold all your family history files, and a similar system of organising 'favourites' or book marks so that you can easily revisit the websites you prefer.

You can obtain back numbers of the SoG quarterly magazine *Computers in Genealogy*, which provides a wealth of information about online family history research. Each issue includes articles, as well as software and book reviews. Appendix 6 shows the index to Volume 6 covering the two years to 1999. You can download more recent contents from the site, and subscribe if you wish.

Additional background and specific information, through articles and special guides, can bring life to the research, and open doors on world and local events and contemporary history. Some information will seem very basic, even to a novice, after a few weeks. Under the 'How To' link, for instance, you will keep coming across the sorts of rules and tips you have already met in Chapter 1. A little repetition, however, can only be to your advantage, as good practice needs to become second nature to get the best out of your research.

3

Harnessing Internet Sources

There are three main sources of family history information on the internet: the world wide web, newsgroups, and mailing lists. Although these have different origins and characteristics, they are accessible through the main operating systems that come with computers and you don't have to know the technical differences to make full use of them.

World wide web websites (with a www address) are for access only through a 'browser', although once into the site you can usually send an email through a 'contact us' link. You can also move by 'hyperlinks' (nerds skip all this ABC stuff) to related websites ad infinitum. Most of the internet source information in this book relates to websites (the world wide web), which is where the vast majority of helpful material resides, and where you can do name searches. Having said that, you can find on websites all you need to know about other ways to use the internet as a resource for genealogy, such as through mailing lists and newsgroups, which we will briefly describe in this chapter.

MAILING LISTS

Mailing lists are discussion forums where people who are interested in a subject can communicate, request and share information, sources, and techniques. There are as many covering family history as on just about any other topic. They operate much like your own email address list to which you can circulate a message to many other email addresses at once. The difference with a mailing list is that everybody gets everybody else's (subscribers') postings, and the list may run to many thousands. 'Replies', likewise, are posted to the entire list. Usually the volume of daily messages is such that for practical purposes you will select to receive a daily or weekly abstract, from which you can access individual messages as you wish. You can, of course, make email contact with people individually rather than via the list once you establish common interests. Like mailing lists about other popular interests, there are a great many covering the subject of genealogy, including specific surnames. So an early task is to check whether there is one or more mailing list for the name you want to research.

From GENUKI and other general FH sites you will find a link to ROOTS-L from rootsweb, which is in effect an electronic mailing list community covering family research and the broader aspects of genealogical research. There are thousands of subscribers, giving you instant access to an enormous resource, including professionals who may frequent the lists. The sites give all the information you need about the specific purposes of each list and any rules to follow, how to subscribe, unsubscribe and so on. Some lists are aimed at novices ('newbies') and these may be of help for a while, but you will be surprised at how soon you become an old hand.

Perusing daily emails, and even just digesting the digests, can take a lot of time. You will therefore need to be choosy as to which ones you subscribe to, and do a regular 'unsubscribe' clean out as soon as you realise you are not getting benefit from a list. Having said that, mailing lists (and websites) rise and fall like empires so it may pay to slip in and out of them to see what they are up to.

Further into your research, more specialised lists will come into their own as you develop particular interests. For example, lists that specialise in different occupations, localities (like FHS lists), specific research guidance such as pitfalls and dead ends, inter-racial ancestry, shipwrecks and persons at sea, and many, many more. Unlike websites, you can post specific queries to a mailing list and draw on the experience of hundreds or thousands of people with similar family history interests.

If you wish you can go straight to a catalogue of LISTSERV lists at www.lsoft.com. Also, the site at www.rootsweb includes 'General Resources on the Internet' and this includes mailing lists, including genealogy-related societies' mailing lists. The rootsweb surname listing includes the strangest names, so there is a good chance you will find yours.

Family history mailing lists

The following are genealogy mailing list links in Cyndi's List (www.cyndislist.com). Go to 'General UK Sites', then 'Mailing Lists, Newsgroups and Chat'. Like everything on this website the lists are long and varied. I have shown this one in full, both to illustrate the range of mailing lists and as a reference list for when your own research might require it:

◇ AUS-CONVICTS Mailing List

For anyone with a genealogical interest in the convicts that were transported to Australia.

◇ BIFHS-USA-NEWS Mailing List

A read-only mailing list for announcements regarding the British Isles Family History Society – USA.

◇ BORDER Mailing List

For anyone interested in genealogy, history, or culture related to the counties which surround the border of Scotland and England. A unique culture evolved in this area which was different from both southern English and either highland or lowland Scottish culture. Many people from the borders were transported to Northern Ireland or left for the colonies.

◇ BR1T-CUSTOMS Mailing List

For the discussion of old British customs and their meanings in relation to British genealogy.

◇ BRITISH-AMERICA Mailing List

The British North America Act of 1867 created the Dominion of Canada. This list explores the 'British' character of Canada and is for anyone with a genealogical, cultural or historical interest in those persons who emigrated to North America during the period of British influence.

◇ BRITISH-CONNECTIONS Mailing List

For anyone interested in British genealogy, history, and culture as well as those who may be seeking connections with relatives or lost friends in the United Kingdom.

◇ BRITISHHOMECHILDREN Mailing List

For anyone who has a genealogical interest in the 100,000 British Home Children – alleged orphans – who were emigrated to Canada by 50 child care organizations 1880–1930.

◇ BRITISH-NOBILITY Mailing List

◇ BRITISH-NORTH-AMERICA Mailing List

For anyone with a genealogical or historical interest in British North America.

◇ BRITISH-VIRGIN-ISLANDS Mailing List

◇ britregiments Mailing List

For anyone with a historical or genealogical interest in British Regiments (including the Indian Army).

◇ BRIT-SURNAMES Mailing List

For anyone researching British surnames. Postings can address individual queries, general research information and needs, and information on existing or planned one name studies.

◇ cayman-connections Mailing List
For anyone with a genealogical or historical interest in the Cayman Islands.

◇ CELTS Mailing List
For the discussion and sharing of information regarding the genealogy, history, culture and religion of the Celts.

◇ CHURCHMEN-UK Mailing List
For anyone with a genealogical interest in church employees (clergy and others) in the United Kingdom.

◇ COALMINERS Mailing List
For anyone whose ancestors were coalminers in the United Kingdom or the United States.

◇ Falklands Mailing List
For anyone with a genealogical interest in the Falkland Islands.

◇ FreeBMD-Admins Mailing List
For discussing, implementing, developing and organising the FreeBMD project.

◇ FreeBMD-News Mailing List
A read-only mailing list for people who are interested in how the FreeBMD project is progressing.

◇ FREEUKGEN-TECH Mailing List
For technical discussions associated with the FREEUKGEN project which exists to bring source material relating to the United Kingdom online.

◇ GENBRIT Mailing List. Gatewayed with the soc.genealogy.britain newsgroup. For the discussion of genealogy in Great Britain and the islands.

◇ Genealogy Aus Convicts Cambridge Mailing List
For anyone with a genealogical interest in the convicts that were transported to Australia on the Cambridge in 1827.

◇ Genealogy Aus Convicts Mary Ann Mailing List
For anyone with a genealogical interest in the convicts that were transported to Australia on the Mary Ann in 1822.

◇ genealogyuk Mailing List
For anyone interested in British Genealogy.

◇ GIBRALTAR Mailing List
◇ HONG-KONG Mailing List
◇ INDIA Mailing List
For anyone who is interested in tracing their British and European Ancestors in British India.

◇ OLD-ENGLISH Mailing List
For deciphering and interpreting documents from the British Isles from earliest times to about 1900. This list is intended for genealogists, family and local historians, etc.

◇ ONE-PLACE-STUDY Mailing List

For anyone who is actively involved in studying a single parish or group of parishes in the United Kingdom as well as those who are about to embark on such a project.

◇ PLANTAGENET-DESCENDANTS-PROJECT Mailing List

For the discussion and sharing of information regarding the descendants of the Plantagenet family who were once rulers of England.

◇ POLICE-UK Mailing List

For anyone with a genealogical interest in former police officers of the United Kingdom.

◇ PRISONS-UK Mailing List

For anyone with a genealogical or historical interest in British prisons and prisoners.

◇ QVDPROJECT Mailing List

For anyone interested in the identification and enumeration of the descendants of Queen Victoria of Great Britain.

◇ RAILWAY-UK Mailing List

For anyone who is researching ancestors who worked on the railways in the United Kingdom.

◇ SOG-NEWS Mailing List

A read-only mailing list for anyone interested in the activities of the Society of Genealogists (of Great Britain), in particular non-members of the Society. This list will be used by the Society to publicise Society events, courses, special library acquisitions, etc. or for comments on genealogical issues.

◇ SOG-UK Mailing List

For the members of the Society of Genealogists (of Great Britain) for topics related to genealogy, the Society resources, or Society issues.

◇ SOUTH-AM-EMI Mailing List

A mailing list for the discussion and sharing of information regarding emigrants from the United Kingdom to South America during the eighteenth and nineteenth centuries.

◇ SURNAMES-BRITAIN Mailing List gatewayed with the soc.genealogy.surnames.britain newsgroup.

For surname queries related to Great Britain.

◇ TRANSCRIPTIONS-UK Mailing List

To share, exchange, acquire or request genealogical data, books, transcriptions, etc. relevant to the United Kingdom, subject to the correct observance of copyright.

◇ ukbooks-announce Mailing List

A read only mailing list maintained by Jodenoy Books, Genealogy Specialists, in association with Amazon.co.uk. Postings by the owners will include news of web site changes and additions, up and coming publications, and other news.

◇ ukbooks-gen Mailing List

For the general discussion of genealogy books. Suitable topics include book reviews; recommendations; and queries regarding hard to find, new, or second-hand books.

◇ UK-CENSUS-CHAT Mailing List

For the volunteers supporting the UK-Census project to discuss project efforts.

◇ UK-CENSUS-COORD Mailing List

For the County Coordinators of the UK Census Transcription Project to discuss day-to-day project activities.

◇ UK-CENSUS-HELPERS Mailing List

For the transcribers and other workers involved in the UK Census Transcription Project to discuss project efforts.

◇ UK-FACHRS Mailing List

For the members of the Family & Community Historical Research Society of Great Britain.

◇ UK-FAMILYHISTORYNEWS Mailing List

A mailing list for the distribution of the Family History News, a newsletter addressing genealogy in the United Kingdom.

◇ UK-GENEALOGY-NEWBIES Mailing List

◇ UK-HISTORY-GROUP Mailing List

◇ UK-ROMANI Mailing List

For anyone with a genealogical interest in Romani (gypsies) in the United Kingdom.

◇ UK-SCHOOLS Mailing List

For anyone with a genealogical interest in old photographs and other information related to schools throughout the United Kingdom.

◇ UK-WATCHMAKERS Mailing List

For anyone with a genealogical interest in watch and clock makers in the United Kingdom.

◇ UK-WORKHOUSE-HOSP Mailing List

For United Kingdom genealogists with workhouse or hospital connections.

Mailing lists are well covered in the multitude of general (non-family history) sites that a 'mailing list' search will throw up, so this is not the place for newbies to learn the basics, simple as they are. The Rootsweb site (*www.rootsweb.com*) referred to earlier gives help on mailing lists generally as well as genealogy ones. The same advice applies to newsgroups, which we will briefly cover next.

NEWSGROUPS

A newsgroup operates on the Usenet worldwide discussion system, distributed through computer networks including the internet. Articles and messages are posted, comprising 'newsgroups'. Usenet is not the internet, which is only one of the various networks carrying Usenet traffic, but the chances are you will gain access to newsgroups via the internet, using the operating system that came with your computer. Popular operating systems, such as Windows, can accommodate both mailing lists and newsgroups, as well as the world wide web. There is a 'list of active newsgroups' published in news.lists.misc.

You can start your own newsgroup (or mailing list), just as millions of people have set up their own websites and this might prove useful if you cannot locate an existing newsgroup featuring the name or topic you want to research – but this is likely to be the exception and will not apply to most readers (i.e. most surnames). Bear in mind that you will need to spend time and effort in doing the basic Getting Started investigation described in Chapter 1, which may bring greater proportionate results – at least for a few months – than breaking new ground on the internet. We shall see in a later chapter also the wealth of information you can get from the Public Record Office.

YOUR OWN WEBSITE

Similar 'take it slowly' advice applies to your own website. Many readers will already have their own or family website, in which case posting your family tree in due course will not take much effort. The mutual advantages of sharing your family history research can be gained through existing genealogy sites, such as ancestry.com and familysearch.com that we covered earlier. So you don't need your own website any more than your own mailing list to use the internet for family history research. By going the ancestry.com or familysearch.org route your ancestral data will be available to the world, and you may gain mutual benefit from other similar or overlapping research without having to set up and administer your own website. A website of your own including all the personal information you wish to display, and photographs of pets and the front lawn, probably has more relevance within your extended family.

FINDING AND USING PROFESSIONALS

The purpose of this book is to give you all the information to do a DIY job. However, some readers may want to hire a professional researcher, perhaps for specific research or because they cannot spare the time personally. Specialised work, such as reading documents in Latin and Old English may be right outside your expertise, although you can add these to your family history aims if and when your research requires it.

You can get advice on most of the main genealogy sites such as GENUKI and the many UK links from Cyndi's list. Various family history journals and newsletters also feature advertisements for a whole range of local searching and more specialised services. Bear in mind, however, that many enthusiasts carry out work free of charge on the basis of 'give and take'. This especially includes visiting a local record office to do a search or collect a certificate that can save a lot of time and expense and is an ideal form of reciprocation. Overseas researchers, such as those from the USA, can benefit particularly, as well as novices who have not yet the expertise to be of much help reciprocally.

There is also scope for people in the UK to share work with someone who lives at a town someone else is researching, in return for reciprocal help. This is where the family history societies (more in Chapter 5) and mailing lists help in putting people in touch with each other. All this keeps the cost down, avoids the need for professionals, and adds to the social aspects of family history as a hobby. Many amateurs who have given many years to their research can provide more expert help than those making a charge. Only by giving as well as taking can such an invaluable network be maintained. Check out the society or email the secretary (see Appendix 2, Help and Support) in your 'target' town to find out what voluntary services can be expected, and how best you can use these and economise on time and effort.

FAMILIA

Familia is a web-based directory of family history resources held in public libraries in the UK and Ireland. It was originally created and maintained by the Family History Task Group of the EARL Consortium. It is now being developed by the Co-East consortia of libraries in the Eastern region.

Familia is the online starting-place to find information about materials in public libraries which will help you trace your family history.

The network known as EARL is a cooperative of local libraries giving listings of local collections of many of the sources used by family historians. This includes much unpublished material that might reveal special insight into the lives of individuals. You can search the GENUKI website to see libraries where census returns, directories, parish register transcripts, electoral registers and unpublished documents are held. Many of these are in printed form, rather than microfiche, so they are simple to access.

Recent collaboration with the Public Record Office (PRO) (covered in Chapter 6) has led to closer links between Familia and the PRO's genealogy website to enable you to get to the information you require quickly. Often sources available in libraries will not be available from record offices, and record offices hold many sources that libraries do not.

FAMILY HISTORY RESOURCES ONLINE

Civil birth, death and marriage records plus the decennial census, and parish records of christenings, marriages and burials, together comprise much of British genealogical research. In the previous chapter we showed how you can access vital records through a couple of top FH websites. These records form a relatively small proportion of the available public records if your interest is in the wider family history aspects. But they are none the less 'vital', especially at the start. However specialised or diverse your research into individual lives, you will need a firm genealogical foundation of names, dates and places to work on.

Census information on occupations, for example, allows you to begin new lines of enquiry from the 'trade or profession' information given, such as records of a possible employer, trade organisation or guild. In such cases, the depth and breadth of research thereafter is potentially unlimited. A book, or specialised website, could never do justice to more than a single main category, such as immigration or emigration, military service, wills and probates, or a geographical area such as an English county. And of these unlimited topics, very few would interest the average reader. Even a book covering a narrow field of genealogy or type of record (and a family history researcher would presumably need umpteen) would soon be outgrown by the available resources for in-depth learning under your own steam. For example:

◆ associating with fellow researchers
◆ visiting local and national record offices
◆ visiting archive depositories such as the Society of Genealogists
◆ exploring specialist websites
◆ doing specific web searches
◆ expanding your knowledge and contacts through mailing lists and newsgroups.

Thereafter, resources are vast and varied and you will need to decide where to branch off, dig deeper and when to acquire special knowledge and experience. The internet resources we cover in the rest of the chapter illustrate the enormous choice you have, and will hopefully remove any mystique from finding your way around and inside the websites.

This is a self-programmed approach to research. It means you not only acquire the basic skills to use internet resources, but that you can expand your skill and knowledge at a pace that suits you. What remains is at least to have an idea up front of the sort of direction your research might take you, the nature of the available records and where they reside. 'Up front' because awareness of the scope and options for research may influence your aims as we discussed in the 'Getting Started' chapter. For instance, you may fancy concentrating on one or more sources, genealogical topics, or geographical areas.

To cover 'genealogical resources' can be little more than a checklist of these many topics and sources. These will guide you, by hypertext links, to where your next enquiries might lead, rather than serve just as a tutorial, or a catalogue of what's available. The aim of this chapter is to fill that need and at the same time whet your appetite as to the sheer richness and variety of sources. It doesn't pretend to do what a specialised record office research will accomplish. There is no such shortcut, and we cover research in the public record offices rather than on the internet in Chapter 8 'Getting to Know Your Ancestors'.

Another purpose of this chapter is to show how you can practically approach any of these myriad topics when you are ready to, and in particular via the internet in the first instance. So as well as providing a checklist of possible doors to further research, it *opens* some doors and gives detailed examples of what you can expect to find on your online exploration.

Fortunately, as we saw in Chapter 2, an initial internet trawl is a fairly standard operation and the process applies well beyond genealogy. Likewise, guidelines on searching are well covered on the respective websites. So, as soon as you have a hands-on try, you will quickly learn how to find what you want, and how to get further help if you can't.

Downloaded world wide web articles, help guides and FAQs cannot cover every eventuality, however, such as how to get a copy of an obituary from a provincial newspaper. But even this and a hundred other specific needs will seem like child's play if you tap into the help of a local family history society, mailing list or newsgroup. If all else fails, a letter, fax or email to the newspaper (in this example) will probably get a helpful reply anyway, without you having to risk abortive journeys. The same common sense approach will work for a hundred other specific needs. In short, once you understand what general and specific resources are available and how to access them, 90 odd per cent of your needs, as an average reader, are covered. The remainder (although I cannot think of instances not amenable to mailing lists or newsgroups world-wide enquiry) will probably require an element of hard experience and skill in any case: in other words, simply giving it a go.

CYNDI'S RESOURCES

Let us now explore a large family history website to illustrate how you can find just about any resource you need by following a standard hierarchical (in fact, hypertext) process. This can be either to learn what's out there – the many potential areas of family history information – or to explore something specific you have in mind. I adopt a hands-on, 'warts and all' approach that will illustrate the pitfalls and limitations as well as 'hits' and practical benefits.

The choice and scope is vast, and Cyndi's List (www.cyndislist.com) illustrates this as well as any website. The following is the 'scaled down', 'no frills' version of the main category index. Select 'No Frills' index on the home page.

- ◇ Acadian, Cajun & Creole
- ◇ Adoption
- ◇ African-American
- ◇ America Online – AOL
- ◇ Asia & The Pacific
- ◇ Australia & New Zealand
- ◇ Austria/Osterreich
- ◇ The Baltic States – Estonia, Latvia & Lithuania
- ◇ Baptist
- ◇ Beginners
- ◇ Belgium/ Belgique/ België
- ◇ Biographies
- ◇ Births & Baptisms
- ◇ Books
- ◇ Calendars & Dates
- ◇ Canada Index
- ◇ Canals, Rivers & Waterways
- ◇ Catholic
- ◇ CD-ROMs
- ◇ Cemeteries & Funeral Homes
- ◇ Census Related Sites Worldwide
- ◇ Chat & IRC
- ◇ Citing Sources
- ◇ City Directories
- ◇ Clothing & Costumes
- ◇ Correspondence
- ◇ Cousins & Kinship
- ◇ The Czech Republic & Slovakia
- ◇ Databases – Lineage-Linked
- ◇ Databases, Search Sites, Surname Lists
- ◇ Death Records
- ◇ Denmark/Danmark
- ◇ Diaries & Letters
- ◇ Dictionaries & Glossaries
- ◇ Eastern Europe
- ◇ Education
- ◇ Ellis Island
- ◇ England
- ◇ Events & Activities
- ◇ Family Bibles
- ◇ Famous People
- ◇ Female Ancestors
- ◇ Finding People
- ◇ Finland/Suomi
- ◇ France
- ◇ GEDCOM – GEnealogical Data COMmunications
- ◇ Genealogy in the Media

◇ Genealogy Standards & Guidelines
◇ Genetics, DNA & Family Health
◇ Germans from Russia
◇ Germany/Deutschland
◇ Greece
◇ Handwriting & Script
◇ Handy Online Starting Points
◇ Heraldry
◇ Hispanic, Central & South America & the West Indies
◇ Historical Events & People Worldwide
◇ Hit a Brick Wall?
◇ House & Building Histories
◇ How To
◇ How To – Tutorials & Guides
◇ Huguenot
◇ Humor & Prose
◇ Iceland/Ísland
◇ Immigration & Naturalization
◇ Internet Genealogy
◇ Ireland & Northern Ireland
◇ Italy/Italia
◇ Jewish
◇ Kids & Teens
◇ Land Records, Deeds, Homesteads, Etc.
◇ Languages & Translations
◇ LDS & Family History Centers
◇ Libraries, Archives & Museums
◇ Lookups & Free Searches by Volunteers
◇ Lost & Found
◇ Loyalists
◇ Lutheran
◇ Luxembourg
◇ Magazines, Journals, Columns & Newsletters
◇ Mailing Lists

◇ Maps, Gazetteers & Geographical Information
◇ Marriages
◇ Medical & Medicine
◇ Medieval
◇ Mennonite
◇ Methodist
◇ Microfilm & Microfiche
◇ The Middle East
◇ Migration Routes, Roads & Trails
◇ Military Resources Worldwide
◇ Mining & Miners
◇ Money
◇ Movies, Music, Fiction & Non-Fiction
◇ Myths, Hoaxes & Scams
◇ Names
◇ Native American
◇ Netherlands/Nederland
◇ Newsgroups
◇ Newspapers
◇ Norway/Norge
◇ Novelties
◇ Obituaries
◇ Occupations
◇ Odds & Ends
◇ Oral History & Interviews
◇ Organizing Your Research
◇ Orphans
◇ Passports
◇ Personal Home Pages Photographs & Memories
◇ Poland/Polska
◇ Poorhouses & Poverty
◇ Ports of Departure
◇ Ports of Entry
◇ Postcards
◇ Presbyterian
◇ Preservation & Conservation
◇ Primary Sources
◇ Prisons, Prisoners & Outlaws

◇ Professional Researchers, Volunteers & Other Research Services
◇ Public Servants
◇ Quaker
◇ Queries & Message Boards
◇ Railroads
◇ Recipes, Cookbooks & Family Traditions
◇ Religion & Churches
◇ Reunions
◇ ROOTS-L & RootsWeb
◇ Royalty & Nobility
◇ Scandinavia & the Nordic Countries Index
◇ Scanners
◇ Schools
◇ Scotland
◇ Scrapbooks
◇ Search Engines
◇ Ships & Passenger Lists
◇ Societies & Groups
◇ Software & Computers
◇ South Africa/Suid-Afrika

◇ Spain, Portugal & the Basque Country/España, Portugal y El País Vasco
◇ Supplies, Charts, Forms, Etc.
◇ Surnames, Family Associations & Family Newsletters
◇ Sweden/Sverige
◇ Switzerland/Suisse/Schweiz
◇ Taxes
◇ Timelines
◇ Travel & Research
◇ Unique Peoples & Cultures
◇ United Kingdom & Ireland Index
◇ United States Index
◇ Video & Audio Tapes
◇ Volunteer Online Regional Projects
◇ Wales/ Cymru
◇ Web Rings for Genealogy
◇ Weights & Measures
◇ Western Europe
◇ Wills & Probate
◇ Writing Your Family's History.

This may appear comprehensive but it is in fact a very high level index indeed. I have omitted some subheadings that have their own A-Z search indexes. The 'Personal Home Pages', 'Societies and Groups', 'Surnames, Family Associations and Family Newsletters' and 'Libraries, Archives and Museums' are cases in point. The USA and UK headings likewise take you to several pyramids of hypertexted resources.

For example, choose 'Societies and Groups' and click down a couple of levels. First to 'General Societies and Groups', then down to 'National Societies' (you could have chosen 'Ethnic Organisations', 'Military Societies' or 'Religious Organisations') and you get:

- The American Historical Association
- Association of Professional Genealogists – Denver, Colorado
- Australasian Federation of Family History Organisations Inc.
- Canada's National History Society
- Dead Persons Society – Australia
- The Federation of Family History Societies – U.K.
- Federation of Genealogical Societies U.S.
- The Institute of Heraldic and Genealogical Studies – U.K.
- National Genealogical Society – Arlington, Virginia
- National Railway Historical Society
- National Trust for Historic Preservation – U.S.
- Nederlandse Genealogische Vereniging
- Society of Australian Genealogists
- Society of Genealogists, UK
- Sveriges Släktforskarförbund/ The Swedish Federation of Genealogical Societies.

As you see, a few of these are UK sites including the Institute of Heraldic and Genealogical Studies that we have not covered in the book and others that we have. The others may contain valuable information about a source type or historical slant, and may even have UK links. You cannot tell from the main index description.

As well as genealogical organisations, Cyndi's List is a good enough place to find a checklist of potential records and source types. A typical high-level index under 'Topical Index' (on the home page), then 'Records', for instance, lists the following:

- Adoption
- Marriages
- Archives – *See: Libraries, Archives & Museums*
- Biographies
- Births & Baptisms
- CD-ROMs
- Cemeteries & Funeral Homes
- Census Related Sites Worldwide
- Citing Sources
- Databases – Lineage-Linked
- Databases, Search Sites, Surname Lists
- Death Records
- Diaries & Letters

- Family Bibles
- Immigration & Naturalization
- Land Records, Deeds, Homesteads, Etc.
- Libraries, Archives & Museums
- Marriages
- Military (see below)
- Newspapers
- Obituaries
- Orphans
- Passports

- Poorhouses & Poverty
- Primary Sources
- Railroads
- Schools
- Ships & Passenger Lists
- Taxes
- U.S. Census
- U.S. – Vital Records
- Vital Records – *See: Primary Sources*
- Wills and Probate.

You will notice that this is also US biased. But there is so much available within these pyramids of hypertext that applies both to the topic generally (such as articles) and to the UK (where many Americans focus their family history work) that it would be a pity to throw out the baby with the bath water. Specific US links such as US vital records can be ignored, of course (unless you are searching emigrant family lines to the USA), but others such as 'Biographies' deserve a deeper dig.

For example, click 'Biographies' and you get the following:

- American Life Histories: Manuscripts from the Federal Writers' Project, 1936–1940
  These life histories were written by the staff of the Folklore Project of the Federal Writers' Project for the U.S. Works Progress (later Work Projects) Administration (WPA) from 1936–1940. The Library of Congress collection includes 2,900 documents representing the work of over 300 writers from 24 states.
- Bio-Bingers Mailing List
  For any and all who are interested in biographies; finding and/or transcribing them, writing them, the proper source citations, etc. and their relevance to the pursuit of genealogy and history.
- Biographical Dictionary
  Covers more than 19,000 notable men and women.

- biographie-center.com
- Biographies and Histories from Around the World
- Biographies of American Architects, 1897–1947
  Biographical material culled from obituaries originally published in American Art Annual.
- Biography & Genealogy Master Index
  Online searchable database.
- biography-center
  Searchable directory indexing thousands of biographies available on the web.
- Biography.com
  A biographical database from the makers of the A&E "Biography" series.
- Bio-Legacy
  We create personal biographies for yourself and/or a loved one for all generations to cherish.
- Celebrate A Life.com
  Dedicated to capturing and preserving the stories of people's lives.
- Center for Autobiographic Studies
  A non-profit organization dedicated to the creation and preservation of autobiographic works.
- Colonial Hall: Biographies of America's Founding Fathers
- Congressional Biographical Directory
  Biographical directory of the United States Congress 1774 to present.
- Distinguished Women of Past and Present
- Geneabios
  Find online biographies for your genealogy research.
- Infinite Humanity
  Using the tools and resources of the Internet, Infinite Humanity has created the world's first ongoing archive for you to record your presence on this planet for both today and future generations.
- Journeyings: Life Stories and Corporate Histories
- The LifeStory Institute
- Lives, The Biography Resource
  Guide to biography sites on the Web with links to thousands of biographies, autobiographies, memoirs, diaries, letters, narratives, oral histories and more.
- North American Slave Narratives
  From Documenting the American South.
- Universitätsbibliothek TU BS, WBI Recherche
  World Biographical Index. From K.G.Saur Publishing and Braunschweig University Library. This database is based on the fifth edition of the World Biographical Index containing about 2.4 million

short biographical entries for eminent individuals who lived in North and South America, Western and Central Europe, Australia, New Zealand, and Oceania. This edition is also a compiled index to many biographical archives.

◆ Women's Legal History Biography Project
History, biographies, photos and articles about women as lawyers in the United States.

◆ WPA Life Histories
Manuscripts from the Federal Writers' Project 1936–1940 at the Library of Congress.

◆ Writing Your Autobiography
From the About.com genealogy section.

(For 'newbies', anything underlined indicates a hypertext link taking you to another site or level of information. The underlining has been removed from the above).

Once again, ignore the obvious 'US only' sites and see what you find. I clicked 'geneabios' (they are in alphabetical order) which took me to a specialised biography site that introduced itself with the following:

Free Genealogy Biography Database

Our free genealogy database of biography is growing rapidly! Search for ancestors by entering a name or location below to check for your ancestors or surnames, or click on the link to see a list of all genealogy biographies in the database. Add biographies of your ancestors to help others.

The directory includes links to 1000's of online biography sites. You will find links to sites with collections that contain numerous biographies in each collection, and links to individual biographies. Be sure to check out both sets of links, since the individual listings are not included in the collections.

A quick search will indicate the extent to which this or any database is truly worldwide, and, of course, whether your own name surname crops up. A 'free search of a billion names' looked promising until I realised that it linked me to ancestry.com (that we covered in Chapter 2) and the search was of surnames (à la IGI etc.) rather than biographies. In fact the database of biographies looks to be in the hundreds rather than even the thousands, so the chances (even ignoring any US bias) are that most of us would draw a blank. However, if your interest is in a one name study you may be luckier, as you can span the globe and not be tied to your own family tree. And even straight, blood-line genealogists may be interested to read published biographies of their namesakes around the world. Determining the presence of your name on the site will just take a few seconds so you need not get into blind alleys or spend abortive time in your travels around links like these.

'Biography-center' claims thousands of biographies, so may have been a better first try. In fact it claimed 11,291 on the date of my visit. These included a Kurt Alder who was no less than a Nobel prize-winner in chemistry, so my couple of minutes' search was repaid and I confirmed my hope that there must be at least one instance of brains in my world family. All these are online biographies, and every one is hypertexted which is where the internet excels. In theory. In fact many drew a 'cannot open page' blank and some took me back to the home page. Others linked to umbrella sites such as 'Australians', the 'Nobel e-museum', educational networks, history sites and suchlike, plus some quite long stand alone biographies that had found their way to a website. I suppose they would accept the life story so far of a reader's teenage child. But they're worth a search as biographies, for most people, in whatever form, are what family history is all about.

UK links

Best of all for UK family historians are the UK sections of
Cyndi's site. Under 'Topical Index' on the home page,
choose 'Localities', then 'United Kingdom & Ireland Index',
then 'General UK sites'.

Under 'Category Index' you have the following choice of
links:

- Colonies & Possessions
- General Resource Sites
- Government & Cities
- History & Culture
- How To
- Language & Names
- Libraries, Archives & Museums
- Mailing Lists, Newsgroups & Chat
- Maps, Gazetteers & Geographical Information
- Military
- Newspapers
- People & Families
- Professional Researchers, Volunteers & Other Research Services
- Publications, Software & Supplies
- Queries, Message Boards & Surname Lists
- Records: Census, Cemeteries, Land, Obituaries, Personal, Taxes and
  Vital
- Religion & Churches
- Societies & Groups.

From the same 'General UK Sites' page you can also link to
one of the 'Related Categories' links:

- Australia & New Zealand
- Canada
- Channel Islands
- England
- England – Counties Index
- Ireland & Northern Ireland
- Isle of Man

- Scotland
- South Africa
- U.K. – Military
- Wales/Cymru.

Now you are in business and can explore, starting geographically, or by topic or source. As an example, I tried just one of these, 'Libraries, Archives & Museums'. I will show this list in full as you can use it for reference in due course, as well as a source of ideas for further research.

- 24 Hour Museum
  UK Museums, galleries, and heritage sites in a searchable database with contact and visitor information plus links to their web sites where available.
- Archives Hub
  Searchable online descriptions of the various archives held by over a dozen institutes of higher education in the United Kingdom.
- ARCHON – A-Z of Repositories
  - ◇ Channel Islands
  - ◇ England
  - ◇ Isle of Man
  - ◇ Northern Ireland
  - ◇ Republic of Ireland
  - ◇ Scotland
  - ◇ Wales.
- Artists' Papers Register
  Online searchable index of papers and primary sources relating to artists, designers and craftspeople located in publicly accessible collections in the United Kingdom.
- Ashmolean Museum of Art & Archaeology
  - ◇ Ashmolean Museum: Antiquities – Brass Rubbings
    An index to the museum's holdings of brass rubbings from parish churches across England & Wales. Some of the index entries include the names of those memorialized.
- A-Z of Military Museums
  Holdings, locations, and contact information from the official Army web page of the United Kingdom. Particularly rich in information on regimental museums.
- The BP Archive
- BP Archive Unit

- The British Heraldic Archive
- The British Library
- BT Archives
  From British Telecommunications.
- Church of England Records Centre – London
- CURL – The Consortium of University Research Libraries
- Family History Centres in the UK and Ireland
- Family History Library Catalog
  From the FamilySearch web site, an online catalog to the holdings of the LDS Church in Salt Lake City, Utah. Also search for other localities by place name.
  - ◇ Channel Islands
  - ◇ Great Britain
    - England
    - Scotland – *New*!
    - Wales
  - ◇ Ireland
  - ◇ Isle of Man
- Galleries of Justice – Nottingham
  Collections focus on law and policing.
  - ◇ The Rainer Foundation Archive
    Holds the extant records of Associated Societies for the Protection of Women and Children, Church of England Temperance Society, London Police Court Missions, London Haven for Women and Girls, London Probation Committee, Society of Juvenile Courts Probation Officers.
- Guildhall Library Manuscripts Collection
  - ◇ Collage Portal
    An image database containing 20,000 works from the Guildhall Library and Guildhall Art Gallery London.
    - search@guildhall
      Experienced researchers will undertake fee-for-service research in Guildhall Library's collections.
- HM Customs & Excise National Museum
  The museum at Merseyside, England has an associated library which includes resources of interest to the family historian researching their excise officer or customs official ancestors.
- The Hudson's Bay Company Archives
  From the Provincial Archives of Manitoba, Canada.
- Huguenot Library
  At the University College London.
  - ◇ eUCLid – the University College London Online Library Catalog

- John Johnson Collection of Printed Ephemera – *New*!
  At the Bodleian Library, University of Oxford.
- Lambeth Palace Library – London
- LDS Family History Centres in the British Isles. Including Ireland and Scotland
- The Library, Friends House, London
  Holds the central archives of Britain Yearly Meeting of Quakers as well as one of the largest collections of Quaker material in the world.
- Manchester Archives and Local Studies – Manchester
  ◇ Family History in Manchester
- Mander and Mitchenson Theatre Collection – London
- Methodist Archives and Research Centre
  At the John Rylands University Library in Manchester, UK. See the link for Researching your Family History on this site.
- Methodist Heritage in the UK
  Methodist Heritage provides a guide to the main locations in Britain with buildings or sites of particular Methodist historic interest. Includes libraries and other research centres of particular Methodist historic interest. Includes libraries and other research centres with Methodist holdings.
  ◇ Methodist Heritage – Research Libraries
  Select list of libraries and archives in Great Britain with Methodist holdings.
- Modern Records Centre
  The Centre's holdings focus on UK trade union records. It also holds the records of some interest groups and political organisations (including West Midlands), of individuals and business (particularly the motor industry). Hosted by the University of Warwick Library, the MRC holds records of interest to the genealogist regarding trades union membership amongst other topics.
  ◇ Genealogy at the Modern Records Centre
  List of occupations covered by the archives for which genealogical guides are available:
  - Carvers, Picture-Frame Makers and Gilders
  - Compositors
  - House Decorators & Painters
  - Prnting Workers
  - Railwaymen
  - Stonemasons & Quarrymen
- The National Army Museum – London
- National Gas Archive
  Company archive of the Lattice Group which holds the historical records of the UK gas industry dating from the early 19th Century.

- National Maritime Museum
  - ◇ Research
- The Caird Library Manuscripts Collection
  This collection includes personal papers of the famous and powerful, Admiralty and Dockyard records, and the business papers of shipping companies and other non-governmental organisations. Also Crew agreement lists and Certificates of Competency.
- NMM Library Catalogue
- Research Guides from The National Maritime Museum
  A listing of the National Maritime Museum's online research guides to their library and collections and to other related maritime sources.
  - ◇ Research Guide No. A3 – Tracing Family History from Maritime Records
    A brief introduction to maritime records you can use to discover more about your ancestors, family history or famous people. It is intended to help you get started on your research, using the National Maritime Museum's library and archives and other resources outside the museum.
  - ◇ Research Guides – The Royal Navy
    Links to four of the National Maritime Museum's research guides regarding the Royal Navy.
  - ◇ Research Guides – The Merchant Navy
    Links to twelve of the National Maritime Museum's research guides regarding Britain's merchant shipping.
  - ◇ Research Guides – World Wars One and Two
    Links to two of the National Maritime Museum's research guides for their holdings on the World Wars.
  - ◇ Research Guide No. FI – Shipping Companies: Records held by the National Maritime Museum
    This guide lists the shipping companies whose records, or part-records, are held by the National Maritime Collection. These are mainly business records and do not cover operations, voyages or passenger lists.
- Parliamentary Archives: House of Lords Record Office
  The archive service for both Houses of Parliament and facilitates public access to several million records which are preserved in the Victoria Tower repository. The records include original Acts of Parliament from 1497, Journals from 1510, papers laid before Parliament from 1531, Peerage papers from 1597, Judicial papers from 1621, and plans of canals, roads, railways and other public works deposited in connection with private bills from 1794. Amongst the comparatively few records of genealogical interest are the Protestation returns of 1642 and certain Papist returns.

- The Public Record Office Home Page
  - ◇ About the Family Records Centre
  - ◇ Family History
- Public Record Office – Easy Search
  - ◇ Public Record Office Catalogue
    These are descriptions of over 8 million documents in the Record Classes of the PRO. The scope and content of the Record Classes are described along with a link to Class List and further links to descriptions of the individual Class Listings. The visitor may either search or browse through the descriptions. Be sure to acquaint yourself with the various nuances and nuisances of the PRO's new facility by visiting
- Frequently Asked Questions
- Glossary
- Hints and Tips
- Search Tips.
  - ◇ The Latest News on the 1901 Census
    Updated accessibility information for the 1901 census online from the Federation of Family History Societies.
  - ◇ Public Record Office Census
    The 1901 census for England and Wales was taken on 31 March 1901 and the census returns will be made available to the public from the first working day of January 2002. For the first time, the census returns 'will be available electronically, via the internet, on this web site.
- 2001 Census project Fact Sheet
- Project News
- The 1891 pilot
- Introduction to the Leaflets
  - ◇ Censuses of Population 1801–1891
  - ◇ How to Use: The 1841 Census
  - ◇ How to Use: The 1851 census
  - ◇ How to Use: The 1861 Census
  - ◇ How to Use: The 1871 Census
  - ◇ How to Use: The 1881 Census
  - ◇ How to Use: 1881 Surname Index
  - ◇ How to Use: The 1891 Census
  - ◇ How to Use: Additional Census Finding Aids.
  - ◇ Public Record Office – Finding Aids – A-Z Index of All Leaflets
- Births, Marriages and Deaths
- British Army Index
- Family History in England and Wales

- Genealogy Before the Parish Registers
- Public Records Outside the Public Record Office
- Royal Air Force Records: Tracing an Individual.
- The Post Office Archives and Record Services
- Project EARL – Connecting Public Libraries to the Network
- Ragged School Museum
  The museum resides in three canal-side warehouses in Copperfield Road, East London. These buildings were previously used by Dr Barnardo to house the largest ragged school in London.
- Repositories of Primary Sources – Europe – United Kingdom
  A list of links to online resources from the Univ. of Idaho Library, Special Collections and Archives.
- The Royal Bank of Scotland Memory Bank – U.K.
- Royal Commission on Historical Manuscripts
  Information on manuscript collections relating to British history.
- The Royal Marines Museum – Hampshire
- The Royal Naval Museum ~ Portsmouth
    ◇ Library
    ◇ Manuscript Collection
    ◇ Oral History Collection
    ◇ Photographic Collection
    ◇ WRNS Collection
    ◇ Wolfson Research Centre.
- Survey of Jewish Archives in the UK and Eire – *New*!
  From the University of Southampton Libraries.
- Trades Union Congress Library Collection
  From the University of North London.
- UK Archival Repositories on the Internet
- UK Heritage Railways
  These pages are intended to provided a guide to all heritage railways, preserved locomotives, preservation societies and railway museums in the UK.
- The UK Public Libraries Page
- University of Essex – The Data Archive
- Wellcome Trust – History of Medicine Library – *New*!
    ◇ Collections – *New*!
- Where are all the UK Record Offices?
- Working Class Movement Library – Salford, England
    ◇ The Boilermakers Monthly Reports – a source for the family historian
    ◇ GMB Britain's General Union – an archive
    ◇ Shipwrights Records in the Library
    ◇ Trade Union Archives.

With all this volume, you are still at 'index' level but just a click or two away from a wealth of information. It would pay to spend a while just exploring some of these links, especially those you think you would like to research deeper. Or random links may give you ideas for research you had never thought about.

Get as much as you can from these world wide web resources. You can use them in different ways:

◆ As a checklist of types and sources of records where you can search for possible ancestors

◆ As a self help resource covering the many aspects of family history it was impossible even to mention in 'Getting Started' and in which you may want to build up some knowledge

◆ As a source of help to follow up leads you have about the lives of particular ancestors you got from living family members, such as their occupation or religious affiliation

◆ As an up-to-date guide to record offices, libraries and museums and other major archive organisations via links to their own websites

◆ As a handy world wide web 'first base' when you have a specific problem (safely remembered in your 'favourites'). The chances are that there will be more than one route to an answer; for instance via a record office or general site and its catalogue or, more directly (but more hit-and-miss), via a more specific archive repository site that may have just what you are after.

EXPLORING DEEPER AND WIDER

Once into any of these sources, your route from then on will differ a lot. In some cases you may be able to search an alphabetical index embracing a whole range of record types. In other cases you will find indices, but by narrower record types, so you will have to repeat your name search in each one. In other cases your first enquiry facility will refer not to a surname, but to a place, organisation or trade, perhaps. Thereafter, your potential enquiry routes will be even more varied and – although in the extreme – will involve no less than poring over unclassified original or microfilmed documents, just as if you received a box of old papers on your initial enquiries among relatives. In this case time planning is very difficult and culs de sac – they come with FH territory – will be more common. Conversely, it is when off the beaten track that you will find treasures of information that may otherwise have been lost forever. At this stage you will find less help is available in your local society, so you may have to focus more on mailing lists and newsgroups world wide, plus specialist societies and organisations. Help, none the less, is still within reach.

In some cases your enquiries will continue within the site, such as through a catalogue hierarchy and/or name search, but almost invariably you will not have access to facsimile records online. So the website is no more than another signpost that confirms where you can go next, whether to a type of record or specific document. Even the vital record searches we covered in Chapter 2 just confirm the existence of a record and you are left to view or obtain a copy in the physical world. Nevertheless, a full use of online resources will multiply your efficiency and save unproductive expense and effort.

At this stage you may have no choice but to make a visit to wherever the records are located, after making the preparation we covered in 'Getting Started'. In other cases you will be able to request information and copies of documents by post, paying online by credit card. As well as catalogues of records these websites usually give all this information, or at least email and telephone contact details. Get into the habit of first, trawling the website for help, whether specific or general, and second, of asking for help through 'contact us' email or telephone help lines.

If you get to the point where you feel you have exploited what the internet has to offer, remember that it is growing apace and a site you visited a year ago may have grown out of all recognition, whilst new ones have come into existence. Linked to this, the hobby itself seems to be mushrooming and there are more and more people out there to form a mutual, completely global family history resource.

You don't have to start with Cyndi's List. I used it because the enormous size helps to illustrate the scope and volume of internet resources. For example, GENUKI will do a similar job, as will the BBC family history website sections or the Society of Genealogists. Anyway, there is a mass of overlap and of the main sites we have featured each does certain things better than the others. So it is worth shopping around, and revisiting a website as a matter of course every few months.

4

Tearless Transcribing

Whether you go the genealogy or family history route you will have plenty of writing to do, in particular copying from one document to another, or transcribing. As you might imagine, this has particular importance in the very nature of the job, especially when transcribing from original records that you may not see again. Many of the problems that today's family history researchers face are concerned with transcription errors on the part of genealogists in the past. I have already mentioned, for example, that we cannot rely totally on databases such as the IGI, and even less on the privately amassed genealogical information posted to the internet. A very large percentage may be accurate, such as perhaps is the case with the IGI and the LDS Family Pedigree databases, but that doesn't help if yours is the one entry that happens to be wrong. You need only one error affecting the name you happen to be searching to really mess up your results, and maybe take you down a road of wasted time and effort.

'Rules' about transcription, and making and keeping records in general, are not just to produce neat looking reports. They are crucial to the 'integrity' of whatever you publish or leave to posterity and, in the long run, to the pleasure you will get out of the hobby. That said, the few guidelines in this chapter, although no more than common sense, may be worth their weight in parish registers in terms of the time, effort and money that good recording can save you.

In a general sense, transcription refers to anything you transfer from one record to another, including keying in data to a proprietry database, such as Microsoft Access, or a proprietary family history program. It may refer, for example, to scribbled notes you got from a distant aunt, either on a visit or over the telephone. In this case, you may not be able to get the information verbatim, so it is important to get facts right – especially names and dates. As far as possible record what you hear or see written rather than what you expect to see or hear or would like to see or hear.

Transcription may also refer to taking extracts, such as from a will you located at a record office. In this case you have to decide what to transcribe – especially from a long document of unknown value – as well as making sure you get it right. If possible take a photocopy, of course. Deciding what to record comes with experience, although the general rule is to record more rather than less as you can never foresee the value of information some time in the future, in conjunction with other data from other sources. There is no reason why, however, by following simple guidelines, you should make all your actual transcriptions right from day one.

With the exception of seasoned professionals, who probably learnt from hard lessons and unforgiving bosses, few researchers maintain complete objectivity. This especially applies when you are researching your own family, as there may be emotional factors. But you can go a long way towards professionalism and objectivity by simple preparation. For example:

- allow yourself enough time
- get your directions to the place, office hours, parking facilities and such like sorted out before you set off
- check the batteries in your recorder if you use one
- book ahead with the record office if you need to (sometimes there are limited places) and request or download helpful information
- decide on specific questions to ask or information to search for
- design pro forma sheets that will capture all the information you may find
- try to get a more experienced person – say from the local FH society – to accompany you first time round.
- have some sharp pencils (ballpoint pens are usually not allowed).

With pre-printed sheets you not only have a checklist of the fields you need to complete, but you have no excuse to use bits of paper that are more likely to get lost. The idea is to make even the most complex transcription task routine and as foolproof as possible.

In the case of transcribing from one written document to another, say at a public record office, there are not as many variables as when recording the highly subjective spoken memories of an aged relative or written material in letters or diaries. However, there may be other pressures, and each kind of research has its own caveats. In a library or record office, time can fly and you may have to rush to beat closing time hoping to avoid another long journey. And that ignores the mesmeric effect of poring over kilometres of hardly legible, microfilmed copies of parish records. We are only human with limited concentration. Most people overestimate the amount of information they will obtain, say in an afternoon, especially when starting off. That applies even when you know that the information is physically available. Once you get familiar with the 'system', using microfiche and microfilm viewers, and the old fashioned style of writing and spelling, your time planning will get better. Otherwise just don't make a time consuming mistake more than once.

The trick, in fact, is simple: start off right and you will establish the right habits. You will soon come to record a certain range of data in a certain way without really thinking about your method. You thus spare your attention for the *content* – such as spelling and dates, plus little clues about relationships you can easily miss and which add to the fascination of the hobby.

All this advice covers record taking generally, including spoken family reminiscences, which, as we have seen, is where we need to start. However, most of your preliminary work will concern transcribing a known, limited range of data (or fields) from a few kinds of 'vital' records, such as parish registers for baptisms, marriages and burials. These recurring transcription tasks will account for a large part of your activity, especially in the early months when you are establishing your main family trees. A standardised 'system' for each main type of record, will therefore repay itself immeasurably. The advice in this chapter covers perhaps 80 per cent of the transcription work you will do, without filling a whole book, which in any case could never address more than a small fraction of the sources out there. For the rest of the more or less unlimited sources, you need to follow the general guidelines in this chapter and rely on good habits created sooner rather than later.

MAKING ASSUMPTIONS

A few simple ground rules are worth indelible mental noting. First, make some assumptions:

- Assume you will not get round to neatly writing up rough notes, and if you do, by then you will have forgotten what some of your notes and abbreviations mean.
- Assume you will not revisit the record office or the place where you have located original documents. In other words, get everything right first time. Don't miss important information that you may never get another go at.
- Assume you will completely discontinue your research at some time, so that whatever you have compiled to that point will need to be comprehensible for someone else – maybe in your family – to carry on if they wish. Scrappy records will not only make life harder for anyone who wants to take the research further, but your own effort will have been wasted if you aimed to leave something of value to posterity. Even though it may not be a serious hobby, it makes sense to keep to simple guidelines. Done well, even very limited research, such as getting to know all you can about a great, great grandfather will be of potential permanent value.

◆ Assume you will forget anything you thought about when actually transcribing. That includes abbreviations that make perfect sense at the time but are no more useful to you than cuneiform a few months later, let alone to someone else. Act as though you simply *don't need a memory* – scrupulous records become the only 'memory' you need. The same applies to ideas that come to you about possible relationships between ancestors, interesting new lines of enquiry and such like, or anomalies and uncertainties that have to be corroborated ('I must check that out'). Make clear notes of insights and brainwaves. It is always worth a few extra words to avoid ambiguity.

◆ Assume you will lose any note that is not part of a permanent record system. So scraps of paper are out. Pro forma, columnar sheets can apply to most recurring records, and these will always be in batches or files rather than single sheets of paper. For non-standard notes and ideas, a hardbound day-to-a-page diary can cover times and places as well as specific sources and 'mental' aides-mémoire.

◆ Assume you will forget research that produced no hits (i.e. targeted records). That means making a record of everything you search, not just everything you find. That way you will not spend hours poring over the same records a year or two later, wondering why it all seems a bit familiar. Eliminating a source or range of records means you are one more source nearer to finding what you want. Think like a detective who patiently 'eliminates a person from their inquiries'.

FIELDS

When designing pro forma sheets to enter basic data, allow for the differing range of fields from place to place and over time. For example, censuses and parish records have included successively more information at a few dates since their introduction, so that as a rule the most recent records are more likely to reflect the possible range of entries to transcribe. For example, a present day birth certificate will come close to what you will need as your standard, or pro forma record sheet.

The exceptions relate to additional fields that make the data more amenable to analysis and re-presentation in reports. For example, by adding a date field in yyyy/mm/dd format you can easily sort records into strict date order – something that you cannot depend upon, say, in bound parish registers, even if supposedly maintained like a diary.

Another important extra field is a place for 'notes' on a record or event. This is like the 'miscellaneous' or 'other' category in forms and questionnaires, and accommodates anything that the other boxes don't. As well as personal historical information in addition to the genealogical 'facts', this is where you can add those long strings of Christian names that can never fit into a standard field, or squeeze into the 'name' column or box on your sheet.

Another obvious blueprint for standard record-taking is the range of fields in a popular family history computer program, designed just with that purpose – every eventuality – in mind. In short, a single form of record can apply to each main category of vital genealogical information: births, baptisms, marriages, deaths, burials. Make everything routine. Plan for surprises and exceptions.

Another fundamental rule is to organise your work so that transcription is kept to the absolute, logical minimum. This seems contradictory to the earlier general rule of more rather than less information. However, 'less' means, for example, avoiding whole intermediary transcription stages rather than trying to make record-by-record short cuts. Every transcription between an original source document and your database means duplication, and that means time, effort and expense – it is what bureaucracies are made of. But this rule makes even greater sense. Each transcription increases the chances of errors between the original 'true' source and whatever form in which it is eventually presented. And, as in the 'Chinese whispers' game, the chance of error increases disproportionately with each extra intermediary record. Hence the growth of point-of-sales (POS) data capture in stores (which has the added advantage of excluding human transcribers). Likewise the use of portable computers to transpose raw, source data to a central, or core database, however the data is later used for different purposes. Whilst still involving fallible human intervention, it eliminates what might have been one or more extra stages of manual transcription with the attendant errors. Go for more content, but fewer error-prone transcription stages. Better, for example, to transcribe straight from a facsimile certificate of a birth, marriage or death into your FH program database, rather than from notes taken from a microfiche viewer. Likewise, importing a GEDCOM file into your program is better than keying in data from a screen entry or printout, assuming of course that you can verify the GEDCOM data.

LIFETIME LOGIC

There are checks one can apply to data once captured that relate to its internal logic. For example, there will normally be a chronological succession of birth, then baptism, then marriage, then successive births, then death then burial. So, all things being equal, your dates should follow this sequence. Similarly, given a few generations of statistics, there are reasonable periods before and after which a woman doesn't bear children. These logical checks can be as valuable in geneaology as getting the number of noughts right when using a calculator, and just as easily got wrong. It's the 'common sense' rule. In particular, you will find yourself guessing at the number of years from one generation to the next, for instance to approximate the date range for a parent's birth in relation to the children. The average is about 25 to 30 years so over 350 years you will span some 12 generations. It is not unusual to find family photographs with four or even five generations together, from 80 year oldish gran to the first newborn of a new generation.

There are exceptions, of course, and these averages just apply in the long run. For example, you may come across very young parents in your search, whatever generation. Similarly, children are born to fathers of a ripe old age. Going back a few generations, gaps of more than a couple of years between children usually meant a stillborn or very early death, or an unrecorded child. A longer period between children might mean the death of the mother, divorce and remarriage. Family planning is a relative innovation. We shall see later that the period between birth and baptism also produces a few anomalies.

All this involves simple detective work but detective work all the same. So treat any post hoc, 'logic' checks ('That's impossible, he could not have been born') as long stops only. Better to ensure accuracy while you have the originals, or films or copies of them, right in front of you than resort to guessing, however clever. You can never guarantee any document is accurate, of course, as humans created them, but by applying the above rules you can get quite close to eliminating mistakes within your own stewardship.

VITAL INFORMATION

Vital information about baptisms, marriages and burials, and later about births and deaths will probably account for a large part of your transcription work. Such data is sufficiently standardised to lend itself to routine, systematic recording using pro forma, pre-printed sheets as we discussed earlier. Significant changes in the kind of information given in vital records over the centuries are very few. From the introduction of parish registers in 1538 which gave basic name, place and date information, the next change was in 1813 when the father's occupation and abode were added to baptisms, and the abode and age, and sometimes occupation, added in the case of burials. Then, at the same time that civil registration was introduced in 1837, age, abode, father's name and occupation were added to the parish records.

Basically you will be recording *fields*, such as a date, name or place or items of data, within a record of an event. Each kind of event, such as a baptism or burial, has its own sort of data items and thus fields. The fields you need to record are more or less the information that is available in the different records, plus, as we saw earlier, any additional fields for notes and to help later analysis. If you use a standard pro forma, or columnar record sheet, some boxes, such as for the father's occupation, will remain empty in the case of earlier parish records. The later registers were themselves pre-printed with columns of information including an entry number, so you don't need much ingenuity to design a standard sheet to capture all the information.

Here is what you may find for a baptism and which will form your record pro forma:

Entry Date	parish	baptism name date	sex	father name	mother name	father surname	abode	trade/ description.

Here is what you might see in a microfiche original register:

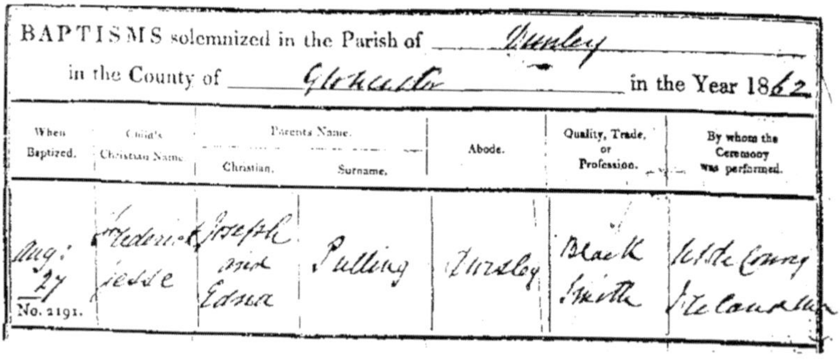

FIGURE 8   Parish baptismal record.

To these basic fields you will need to add information that may be shown, even though not required by statute, such as a birth date in the case of a baptism record, or a mother's surname. Individual parish priests and clerks might give this additional information in one of the boxes or the margin. In designing a standard record sheet you will also need a place for notes (or a cross-reference place to a hardbound notebook that can accommodate notes of any length), a sort date as described earlier, and other fields depending on what you may want to do eventually with your information, or what your software program caters for.

Repetition

Keep repetitive transcription down to a minimum, such as when recording the name of the parish which applies to a whole batch of records. This item is not shown on the early registers and it is tempting to miss it out anyway as it repeats itself. This is fine when completing your pro forma sheets at the public record office, but not when entering the data into a computer database. That's because you may need parish information later, such as when combining two sets of records, which you can then differentiate and later search by parish. But you can save time by abbreviating the parish name, such as ks for Kingstanley, then simply doing a 'find and replace' edit that will make all the changes at a stroke. That's a useful trick whenever you have repetitive information to transcribe. It is one case where abbreviation makes sense as it optimises your time at the record office.

Date format

Get the date format right from the start and keep to it throughout your genealogical career. The most common format is dd mmmm yyyy/y – for example, 23Feb1770/71. This way there will be no misunderstanding between day and month as exists between the US and UK date forms, or for any other reason. The /y at the end will only apply when a 'double date' applies – that is, a date before March 26th in the period when the year number changed on March 26th rather than January 1st (below). Even though such entries may be relatively few, the rule is to allow for all possible variants of an entry when designing your database. The popular family history software programs will have their own date system, or require you to choose, which you should check before entering data. Fortunately the better programs are fairly idiot proof, but an understanding of the significance of dates is necessary anyway and you are going to meet 'double dates' sooner or later. You will also meet US format dates in some contexts so don't forget the logic check above, and the need to corroborate all data.

Double dates

From 45 BC many parts of the world used the Julian calendar in which each year started on 25th March and a year lasted for 365 days and 6 hours. Pope Gregory XIII was concerned that the calendar was getting out of kilter with the natural years and so the so-called Gregorian calendar was introduced in 1582. This changed the first day of the year to 1st January and also skipped 10 days to make up for the lost time over the centuries. 2nd September 1752 was followed immediately by 14th September 1752. Some people added 11 days to their birth date, although this would not appear on the parish or public records.

Not all countries used the new calendar from the same date so what is called double dating relates to this overlap period.

England did not officially accept the new calendar until 1752. Before that date, while the government used 25th March as the new year date, most of the population observed 1st January, so for some years people wrote both dates when recording a date between 1st January and 25th March. In fact many people continued to write double dates for years after the official change so if you are dealing with this period you are likely to come across this. Most, however, have been corrected to the present calendar when captured in genealogical databases.

Sex

The sex of an ancestor may seem superfluous when names are given, but of course, even today, you cannot be certain. My friend Julian is male, but Julian used to be a female name and such examples abound. Bear in mind that what is normal today may have been abnormal a couple of centuries ago, and the same applies to different parts of the world in the same historical period. This follows the simple rule that there should be no room for ambiguity.

Names

Confusion can also occur when first names seem like surnames and vice versa. To overcome this potential ambiguity the tradition is to use capitals for a surname. But that doesn's mean that a previous transcriber applied this, or any other protocol! However, by adopting this simple habit you are almost certain to make life easier for yourself at some later date or for anyone else referring to your records.

The father's and mother's 'names' in the above baptismal record illustration are first, or Christian, names. The absence of a father's name does not necessarily mean the child is illegitimate – he (the father) could have died. A description 'single woman' under the trade/description heading is a more likely indicator of illegitimacy.

If there is not enough space for three or more first names, you can resort to your 'notes' field. In most software programs this field is as big as you will ever need, so it will accommodate biographical data and research queries to any degree. If building your own database (such as with Microsoft Access) use a 'memo' rather than text field, as the latter is very restricted in characters.

Notes

The Notes field becomes an important part of your database if you wish to focus on in-depth family history rather than just names and dates. For example, it could incorporate verbatim text of letters to or from the person, a will or excerpts, gravestone records, a helpful email message from a fellow researcher or family member, and so on. Bear in mind that the Notes field will not be amenable to further analysis as applies to specific data fields – it's just a lot of text. It pays therefore to utilise standard fields to the maximum, such as for second and subsequent given names, previous marriages or name changes. Most family history software packages cater for many options.

Abode and Trade

'Abode' is usually a parish or town name, although a full address may appear, or a specific term such as 'workhouse' or 'poorhouse'. This and any explanatory information can also be added to the Notes field, being of potential value later. 'Trade' or 'occupation' denotes 'Quality, trade or profession'.

'Quality' would apply where the father was a 'gentleman', for example, or a description such as 'single woman'.

Age

This general advice will apply to transcribing all three main parish register record types – baptisms, marriages and burials. The content, or nature of the events, changes but the genealogical principles and transcription rules remain the same. One special case, however, is the age at death that may appear on a burial record. This may appear in several forms, and includes very young children whose ages are shown in months, weeks, days or even hours (5m, 5w, 5d, 5h). Also appearing in this column is the enigmatic term 'infant'.

An age may also appear when the age of a child baptised is greater than usual, such as 'aged 6 years'. This is not catered for in the later pre-printed parish registers so will usually appear, if at all, as 'born 30th August 1812' – maybe in the margin. Unfortunately there was no standard practice as to the baptism age above which this would be noted, so a baptism record means no more than that. Hence the usual approximation of birth in genealogical records as being before that (baptism) date (e.g. b bef 6th March 1804). It was not uncommon for two or more children to be baptised on the same day – another example of the approximation involved in birth dates before civil registration was introduced. Adult baptism was not the practice in the Church of England but may apply to West Indian immigrants.

The above cases are the exceptions, of course, and most transcription problems amount to simply reading the handwriting and coping with a poor microfiche copy. Most vital records are straightforward, like the burial record in Figure 9, and you are left with reading only the handwriting.

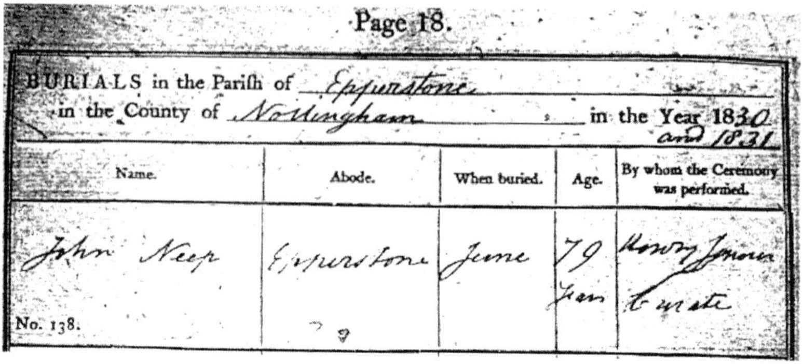
Page 18.

BURIALS in the Parish of Epperstone in the County of Nottingham in the Year 1830 and 1831

Name.	Abode.	When buried.	Age.	By whom the Ceremony was performed.
John Neep No. 138.	Epperstone	June	79 Years	Henry Jones Curate

FIGURE 9 Parish burial record

The important thing is not to read anything into the record but transcribe exactly what is there. The detective work that may suggest further lines of enquiry will come later.

CIVIL BIRTH, DEATH AND MARRIAGE RECORDS

You can find births, deaths and marriages records from 1837, when civil registration was introduced by law, at the local record offices and also at the Family History Centre in London. The FHC indices are alphabetical in quarter years, so that the March 1880 index, for instance, will include events between 1st January and 31st March in that year. If a search is confined to names, dates and places from these indices the same transcription principles as above apply, even though you have less items of data and you are working from a secondary or tertiary (compiled) record rather than from a photographic film of the original. So you can still adopt a routine system, with columns for each item, and allowing in this case a number of records on a pre-printed page. The parish registers continued in parallel with the new civil records, of course, but the latter offers a more complete and perhaps more reliable record.

Back to record basics

In one sense life gets easier as you get closer to the present day, as the difficulty in actually reading early parish registers and interpreting old spelling and abbreviaton practices is almost removed. On the other hand, you may not be working with the source of the record, such as a bound register, and the laws about transcription errors noted earlier will apply. If you obtain copy certificates from the record office, you get back nearer to the source. However, even though the costs are fairly nominal, this can be expensive when, depending on your genealogical aims, the numbers get large. Bear in mind also that the 'certificate' you obtain from the local record office or by post from the central office at Southport may be a typed copy rather than a photograph of the original certificate or register – in other words, another intermediate transcription. So for critical records it is better to get copies of the original document, such as the marriage register, complete with your ancestors' signatures, from the local record office where they are physically held. As well as this being the most authentic document for transcription to your computer database, you then have a facsimile source document to retain as part of your records. For most people, the real McCoy document will bring more affinity to your ancestor than a modern typed version, let alone an index listing. It's best to have a rational, economic policy in all this, to control both time and expense. For example, you might decide to obtain copies of originals for everyone in your direct, surname ancestral line, but rely on online and record office indices for the other branches of the tree.

Civil registration of marriages began in 1837, from which date you could get married in a register office or, if licensed for marriages, a noncomformist church or chapel, or a Catholic church. The new register contained much more information than previously:

- The year
- The place of marriage, including the parish and county
- Register entry number
- The date 'when married'
- Name and surname of groom and bride
- Age of groom and bride
- Condition (e.g. bachelor, spinster, widow, widower)
- Rank or profession (occupation, not usually applicable to a bride)
- Residence (of both groom and bride) at the time of marriage
- Father's name and surname (of both groom and bride)
- Rank or profession of father (of both groom and bride)
- Whether by banns, or licence
- Signatures (or marks) of the groom and bride
- Signatures of two witnesses
- Signature of the person performing the ceremony.

With many more items of data, you now have the luxury of deciding which information you do *not* want to transcribe, and this may follow a similar policy to whether or not you obtain copies of originals. Once again, it depends on where you would like your research to take you, and your aims when setting out. If you want to explore any interesting family history that suggests itself, the names of witnesses, for example, may be part of the story. On the other hand, if your research is limited to genealogical names and dates, you can choose the information fields that will help to *corroborate* such information, such as the ages of the bride and groom and father's surname. A marriage record can help remove uncertainty from data built from indices such as the IGI, or pre-1837 parish baptism registers, especially where the surname is a common one.

5

Organised Support

A few leading genealogy and family history organisations provide a wealth of information and specific help in every aspect of family history. These have their own websites, but the Society of Genealogists differs from the top websites covered in the book in that they have an office in the UK at which you can search extensive physical archives not accessible through the world wide web. As with public record offices, you therefore need to know what is on offer and how you can get the best out of the records. The organisations' sites themselves describe their various services in detail so a brief introduction only is needed here. There are equivalent family history and genealogy organisations in the USA and other countries, and these are also accessible via their websites. Cyndi's List website, as we have seen, has links to all kinds of family history-related organisations. Some are specialised, as you would expect, so an exploration of these is advisable when you have got properly started and have developed some particular interests, or face specific questions. Those featured in this chapter are more general and deserve an earlier visit.

SOCIETY OF GENEALOGISTS (SoG)
www.sog.org.uk

This society has its own archives of records that can be accessed at their office in London and offers a unique combination of research material, guidance and support. It is a charity whose objects are to 'promote, encourage and foster the study, science and knowledge of genealogy'.

The SoG library is claimed to be the foremost in the British Isles with a large collection of family histories, civil registration and census material, and the widest collection of parish register copies in the country (over 9,000). Sections of the library cover the professions, schools and universities, the armed services, religious denominations, the peerage, heraldry, and British citizens living abroad. Boyd's Marriage Index covers some 2,600 parish registers with nearly seven million names. You can search the IGI on both CD-ROM (LDS FamilySearch) and microfiche, and online in the society's computer suite, which offers free access to genealogical sites.

The Society runs an extensive range of lectures and courses on specific topics, to suit beginners right through to those with considerable knowledge. The facilities and events are available to members and non-members alike, but members have free access to the library and discounts on the Society's events and publications. The Society runs two mailing lists, one giving news and information and the other a discussion list for members.

You will find this site particularly helpful when you advance from basic births, deaths and marriages records to other kinds of data and sources. Like all these sites, there is plenty of on-site help, both in finding your way around the site and also in doing your research generally. In this case the site caters for professional genealogists as well as the many lay people who use it. You can print out information leaflets on subjects like:

◆ note taking
◆ the relevance of surnames
◆ employing a professional researcher, and
◆ genealogy as a career.

You can search a name at this site but it links you to GENUKI which we cover later. Another search facility, on the home page, takes you to origins.net, the website of English Origins. This search incurs a small charge and the records are very limited. However, the search facilities at the SoG London offices are extensive, and will often provide a key to a whole direction of research. A visit to the library is invariably the best advice, provided you are well prepared regarding the records you want to see, finding your way around and armed with specific questions. However, you can also obtain information by writing to the Society with your specific enquiry – read up on this on the website first. It is best to explore the website before even considering a visit to the offices.

You can print out some of their general help leaflets, listed below, if you want more guidance and background reading.

◆ Family records and their layout
◆ Note taking and keeping for genealogists
◆ Genealogy as a career
◆ Notes for Americans on tracing their British ancestry
◆ The relevance of surnames in genealogy

- Starting genealogy
- The right to Arms
- Essential addresses
- The Data Protection Act and genealogists
- Has it been done before?
- Employing a professional researcher: a practical guide
- SoG Welcomes your Research.

Bear in mind that most 'getting started' articles and leaflets say much the same thing – like 'talk to your relatives', 'work backwards', 'keep careful notes' and such – so you soon need more specific guidance. Although the site itself may not be the biggest, the SoG as an organisation is a treasury of genealogical information.

The library holdings are too extensive to list in full. The lower library (LL) in the basement is a good place to start as it houses some important indices:

- General Register Office indices England & Wales 1837–1925
- 1881 Census indexes on fiche & CD ROM – 1841–1861 census returns on film
- Scottish GRO indexes 1855–1920
- International Genealogical Index, 1992 edition on fiche
- Scottish pre-1855 OPR indices on fiche
- Scottish 1891 census index on fiche – Scottish 1841–91 census returns on film
- Principal Probate Registry indices 1858–1930
- Pre-1858 will indices & calendars on film
- Great Card Index & film/fiche collections
- Manuscript Document & Special collections
- CD-ROM computers (for IGI etc.)

- Internet Access to Online Databases
- Microforms & Readers
- Closed access items (Apply to staff – except items located on 'shelf 9' or 'fragile binding').

Further information about your ancestors, such as trades and professions and religious affiliation can be researched on upper floors, which also house census and other records.

Computerised cataloguing was introduced in 1991 since when all new acquisitions have been entered. The Library Catalogue Project was begun in 1997 with the aim of computer cataloguing approximately 80,000 items acquired before that date. The project is now complete and OPAC (On-line Public Access Catalogue) terminals are available in all parts of the library. Although not yet online, a county by county list of all the parish registers held in the library appears on the Parish Register copies section of the website. One hundred and five thousand items are listed at the time of writing. Recent acquisitions are listed in the Genealogists' Magazine and the SoG website.

FEDERATION OF FAMILY HISTORY SOCIETIES
www.ffhs.org.uk

This is the umbrella organisation of the local Family History Societies already referred to. It has affiliation with societies and organisations around the world, organises conferences and runs national family history projects. From the FFHS website you can find the contact details of your local Family History Society – see 'Contacting our Members' (don't confuse these societies with the local branch offices of the LDS – Family History Centres). Appendix 2 shows a list of Family History Societies.

Local societies

Society members comprise county and area FHSs in the UK, national, state and province FH organisations worldwide, and denominational and specialist organisations around the world. Just key in the county you are interested in and you will get addresses and contact details. These societies are all over the country and by joining you will immediately access an important resource, whatever your family history aims. You can get lots of local as well as general information from the individual societies' websites and mailing lists.

Joining the society nearest you is valuable for general help, but you will need to join the society or societies in the places your research takes you if you want to use this resource for tracking down specific ancestors. Each society has archives of information regarding ancestry in their area and members usually undertake ongoing work to extend these. For example, you can probably locate a record of memorial inscriptions and cemetery records in the county or area, with a name index. Or you may find that members have done research that overlaps with your own research target. Certain surnames may be concentrated in relatively small areas geographically, more so the further your research goes back, when mobility of workers was the exception rather than the rule. Even if you don't find ready-recorded information on your particular name enquiries, the local society is where you will find information about the place where your ancestors lived. Membership costs typically a few pounds a year.

Mailing lists

If the society has its own email mailing list (covered in Chapter 3) you can subscribe to regular postings or weekly abstracts to keep in touch (your choice will depend on the time you want to spend on reading [or even just opening] them and the size of the list. You can switch at any time to an abstract). For complete computer newbies, I should say that 'subscription' to a mailing list or newsgroup doesn't imply there is any charge.

Resources

Get to know what records are available and let fellow members know your surname interests – a simple posting on the mailing list will do. The society I joined has an invaluable resource compiled by an Australian researcher (non UK residents often have greater knowledge and enthusiasm about their British ancestry) who has built up a database of the many surname studies in the Gloucestershire district. This sort of information, sometimes the result of years of work, can be of special value if you are fortunate enough to come across it. In the above case you can identify the many individual contributors, so you can circulate your own interests to see if work has already been done covering your own family tree. A contributor might reside anywhere in the world, as the town or parish of common interest was perhaps two or three centuries ago. Liaison regarding a name, place or topic may take place via a mailing list or newsgroup or with individual members by email, telephone or post.

Joining an FHS and its email list opens up a potentially unique resource, because of the concentration of local knowledge. This is likely to include occupations, commercial organisations, land ownership and tenancies, epidemics and traditions – in other words, what makes your research family history as well as genealogy. Varied and sometimes large membership also provides a general resource that includes research methods and specialist experience including professional genealogists and researchers. Initially two-way sharing of knowledge will seem to work all in your favour, and as a novice you may feel obligated, but soon you will be able to share your own findings.

An important development has been to transfer information previously in microfiche form onto PC floppy disks and CD-ROMs. You can buy these from the local society and the costs are reasonable considering the enormous work involved in transcription. You may find, for example, that census data for the county has been alphabetically indexed by name and is unavailable from any other source.

The FFHS publishes a series of county genealogical biographies, listing the sorts of printed information published in the periodicals of local archaeological and similar societies that you can find in local libraries. Often the records covered by these sources are very difficult to decipher in the original, such as eighteenth century manor court documents.

One name societies and 'strays'
The site also has a list of one-name societies (you are in luck if your family name has a one-name society) and other genealogy-related societies. Some specialise, such as in Quaker or Jewish records, Romanies, Catholics and heraldic studies. Information is available covering, for example, military personnel records, adopted persons, and 'strays'.

Strays are people who are described in the record as being 'from, or connected with, a place outside the area in which they normally lived.' Compiling 'strays' registers is typical of the varied functions of Family History Societies. The National Strays Index and the Strays Clearing House are examples of the coordination and consolidation functions of the federation.

Members' interests

The Federation produces the British Isles Genealogical Register (known as the Big-R) available via the website. Many local societies publish directories of members' interests (little-Rs) so you can find out who may be already researching your ancestors, a place of interest and specialised areas of genealogy.

Local research services

An advantage of membership of one or more societies is in getting help in doing specific research at a record office in another part of the country. This is mainly a free (in fact mutual, or reciprocal) service although many individuals put in a lot of disproportionate effort. The societies themselves do not usually hold extensive physical records, and most enquiries and search requests relate to records held at their local county records office, to which a member will have to travel and spend time. The system will therefore work only if help is reciprocated between societies and individuals. It also helps if requests are specific and concise, and the federation, as well as individual societies' websites, gives guidelines in this respect.

Each societies' holdings, and the services they offer, vary a lot but the following is the 'Quick Reference' menu on the Gloucestershire FHS home page, which is probably typical:

1851 Census Index – on fiche
1851 Census on CD
1901 Census NEW
Burial and Memorial Sites Index
Electoral Roll Index
Full index of GFHS publications
Gloucestershire Surnames List (published by David
     Steel)
Gloucestershire Burial Index – *New*!
How to join
Items from the GHFS Journal
Marriage Index
Memorial Inscriptions Index
National Burial Index
Officers
Open Days
Overseers of Poor Papers – Name index
Prisoner Registers Index
Resource Centre
Search Services
Smart's Directory of Gloucester for 1910 – *New*!
Strays Index

When you trace recurring births to a parish or local area, it
pays to join the local (or nearest) society, explore their
resources and get in touch with some of their people. A lot of
mutual time and effort can be saved by pooling societies'
resources. For example, if you have a date, a society member
in the town may copy a newspaper article from local
archives. Novices can handle such services, when clearly
specified, so a member soon starts to earn his or her keep
reciprocally.

Some societies do not offer such services, often because the demand for searching in their geographical area outweighs their membership human resources. Population concentration changes over the centuries and some societies are more evangelical than others in attracting members. However, through the journal or directory of members, society members around the country can stay in touch with those doing research into the same family lines. A local society website will usually specify what research can and cannot be undertaken by the society, the private indices they hold, local record office indices held only by the society, and other information. Some societies also carry out searching their archives at a fee, and again the website will give details. The Gloucestershire society will search strays, marriages, the local census and National Burial Index at a charge of £1 for members and £2 for non-members.

Conferences and fairs

The FFHS fosters and supports half-yearly Family History Conferences in the UK, usually hosted by member societies in rotation. The site also lists family history fairs around the country, at which the federation is usually represented, and where their publications will be on sale. A more complete listing of FH fairs can be found on the GENUKI website.

National projects

The federation undertakes genealogical projects at a national level, and is presently concerned with the following:

◆ *1851 Census Indexing* on a county basis, for the remaining counties not yet completed

- *1891 Census Indexing* (and subsequently indexing of the other publicly available censuses) on a county basis
- *Marriage Indices* on a county basis, particularly for the period 1754–1837
- *Monumental Inscriptions* transcription for all church and chapel yards, and public cemeteries on a county basis
- *National Burial Index* on a county and national basis. This covers burials from various written sources such as parish records, rather than from monuments (gravestones). It is ongoing and complements the IGI which is largely restricted to baptisms and marriages. This is mainly an index, and does not include all the information from the source records. The researcher is always advised to refer to the source document which is part of the index
- *National Inventory of War Memorials* (in conjunction with the Imperial War Museum) on a county basis
- *National Strays Index and the Strays Clearing House.* We referred to strays earlier in the chapter. You can find more about these two projects on the FFHS site.

New indices are always of interest to genealogists as they can save a lot of time. You can check with the federation what census and marriage indices are complete, for instance.

GUILD OF ONE NAME STUDIES (GOONS)
www.one-name. org

A one-name study is a project researching all occurrences of a surname as opposed to a particular pedigree (the ancestors of one person) or descendency (the descendents of a person or couple). A true one name study covers the whole world, although some are limited perhaps to one or more countries. The Guild of One Name Studies invites membership from people doing worldwide research, and this is a good way to register your interest in a name and share information. As you will imagine, most names are uncommon, or certainly not the most common, although any name is eligible provided a person can show they intend to research worldwide. A website name search will reveal whether your own name, or one you want to research, is currently being studied by a guild member.

The Journal of One Name Studies is published quarterly and includes information, ideas and articles for members. A register of one name studies is held and there is a Guild email forum (a mailing list, see Chapter 3) offering a permanent email address with your name followed by @one-name.org. Many names are also associated with one name societies and produce a periodical newsletter. Doing your own family research may be lonely until you meet people covering similar territory, so in this way you can quickly establish like-minded people when researching present names world wide. The Guild holds meetings and arranges speakers around the country.

These studies typically identify the distribution of names (say per telephone directories) within a country and throughout the world, its origin, the dominance of particular professions, famous people and so on. The Guild has certain minimum requirements regarding the extent of the research, although for the first category of membership you have to show only that you have made a start and serious intent.

For some, this form of family name activity gives as much pleasure as conducting their own, direct family pedigree.

Depending on how uncommon the name is, such research is always a big task and you will have to take account of the time and expense necessary when setting your aims. That said, you don't have to do a formal study, or work through the GOONS, and can take an interest in your surname distribution in as cursory or shallow a way as you like.

In any event there is plenty of overlap between one name studies and more conventional genealogy and family history, and you are likely to use the same resources and visit the same public offices. Births, deaths and marriages, for example, are obvious sources of surnames and these are often available on microfiche or CD-ROM. Bear in mind that although a one name study can be a formidable task, in practice there will probably be many people involved, even though it was originated by one person, and – as in most projects like this – just a few people may undertake the lion's share of the work. If this takes your fancy you will find all you need to know at the GOONS site, or by contacting them by email at guild@one-name.org.

6

Vital Public Records

Public records are held today on every aspect of our lives, and it wasn't very different in the past. The Public Record Office (PRO) at Kew, in London, houses one of the most complete archives in the world, running unbroken from the Domesday Book in 1086. Appendix 1 shows the online catalogue running into hundreds of source types and record topics, each with a printable information leaflet. Each of these topic headings is hypertexed to information that will help you to prepare for your research at the London office. The Family History Centre holds birth, marriage and death records, as well as censuses (which are not held at the PRO).

Most records are made available for public access 30 years after their final creation. So with the exception of census records which are not available for 100 years, there are no practical restrictions on access for most family history purposes. At one level they open a window onto contemporary social, economic, political and religious history for a millennium, whilst at another level they touch the individual lives of millions of ancestors, including yours and mine.

PURPOSES AND PROCESSES

The records were not produced for family historians. They relate only to times when people came into contact with the government or judicial system, such as when they were registered as born, married or dead, joined the armed services, sold land, were due to pay tax, were criminals and so forth. So it is not easy to find information on a particular person or family unless you know what would have necessitated a record, and the way the records were created or processed. Very few of the records have alphabetical indices by name. Hence the usual start with indexed records of births, deaths and marriages, and the need for as much information as possible from within your family. However, the fact that it is well hidden doesn't mean that information about your ancestors doesn't exist. It means, rather, that you will need knowledge and detective skills to track it down. It is unlikely that anyone but you or someone in your extended family will make such a serious search for ancestors, so this is an opportunity to bring to life personal history that might otherwise have been lost to the world forever.

Whilst everything is expertly catalogued, there is no 'subject' index as such at the PRO, and the records are generally in the categories relating to their multitude of original purposes. To make even reasonable use of the wealth of information available, it is therefore necessary to learn something about the nature and purpose of the various kinds of records. For example, who was responsible for what sort of affairs? Who is likely to have written to whom? What kind of information had to be kept for posterity? and so on. With over 500 km of records on the shelves, there is no practical limit to the depth to which you can investigate your ancestors, and the extent of the learning process. At minimum, this obligatory background knowledge provides an ideal introduction to the history and culture of the periods in question, and putting your ancestors into a context, enabling you to know them better. Whilst most family researchers get by with the minimum of such knowledge, for many this is the main pleasure and challenge of family research. From these disparate records you will understand something of the kind of life your ancestor lived, the domestic, social, economic, industrial and political conditions of the time. Likewise you will see your relations within a backdrop of wars, legislation, religious movements, disasters and so on.

This rich history, including sometimes extraordinary detail of the lives of your own kin – such as in a will or military service record – lies hidden in the records. You don't have to decide up front the extent to which you will dig into all the available records – you will probably first want to gauge the sort of time, committment and expense it will mean. Be prepared to do some real detective work and background learning, however, if you want to bring your ancestors to life and get maximum pleasure as a hobby or worthwhile project. Otherwise your research may amount to little more than geneological trainspotting.

Keep an open mind

Although I concentrate on 'vital' records, where you will usually start, other records are as vast as they are varied. The main index or catalogue, which you can browse through at the office, runs to over 5,000 pages, and the awesome range of the records is illustrated by just a summary index I have added as Appendix 1. You can use this as a check list of possible sources of family history information, as you cannot predict where your ancestors may have appeared in the scheme of things. You may have to explore them one by one. But have an open mind as to what you may discover. Just because you are not a military family does not mean that the same applies to former days. Because you are relatively crime free today it doesn't follow that your folk did not darken the doors of the penal institutions of their day, or even pay the ultimate price. Similarly, just because you have paid off your mortgage doesn's mean that your ancestors stayed free, for whole generations, of the workhouse and bankruptcy courts. And the chances are that some brave souls with your name made a perilous journey to the New World and made some mark in a new land of opportunity.

It is impossible to do justice to these in a single book and most family searchers add to their knowledge as they go on, and as the need arises. None the less, family history as distinct from family trees, is where most of the exciting discoveries occur, and where the first addictive signs usually appear. Chapter 8 gives a flavour of the variety and scope of 'non-vital' public records.

Dig deep and wide

Potential family history data is more or less unlimited and you need to agree some approximate aims before you launch into record office searching, and perhaps to revisit them as you are confronted with new possibilities and decisions at different stages in your research, It is usually better to do a few things and do them well, or, put another way, to dig deep rather than journey wide. Without a plan and sensible preparation, and preferably a few specific questions to answer, you can easily spend whole fruitless days in these national record offices.

As well as the PRO at Kew, the main public records of births, marriages and deaths are held at the Family Records Centre (FRC) in Myddleton Street, London. This is run jointly by the General Register Office of England and Wales (GRO), part of the Office for National Statistics (ONS) and the Public Records Office (they have a floor of the building each). These comprise civil births, deaths and marriages records dating from 1837, legal adoptions from 1927, and census returns from 1841 to 1891. The census records held at FRC are the only main records not held at Kew.

Website resources

The FRC website is *familyrecords.gov.uk*. From there you can find detailed information about the records held, how to find your way around them and obtain certificates, opening times and such like. The addresses and telephone numbers are included in Appendix 4. If you visit the FRC bear in mind that the Society of Genealogists and Guildhall library are not many minutes away so you may wish to make a long day of it and prepare to cover each.

The PRO web site is www.pro.gov.uk and this also offers a wealth of information. In particular, you can search the extensive catalogue of records – for record type (or purpose) rather than content. Having said that there are a few name indices mainly of published biographical records. These are mainly 'important' people but if alphabetical name indices exist, for the sake of a few minutes searching, it is worth using them even if just to eliminate a major source of enquiry. The catalogue of records will start to come into its own as you get clues about specific people, concerning their occupation, tenancy or land ownership, war service or suchlike. For example, you could search for a nurse or hospital worker from hospital records.

Here I will give a brief summary to help you on your first search at the offices. After your first session and a few teething troubles (however well prepared you think you are) you will find it easy to obtain the basic B, D & M records. The PRO has a vast range of additional records and I have shown the master index (it is also a list of information leaflets) as Appendix 1. Searching these is covered in Chapter 8. In any event it is always advisable to consult the website of a record office or library before making a visit. As well as being sure you will find it open, and checking on any parking provision, you can usually get a good idea of the layout and helpful searching tips, and in some cases consult a catalogue of records to prepare more specifically. All this preparation increases *productive* time when you get there, as well as sparing you the inevitable, odd abortive day trip. It rarely pays to make a long trip unless you are quite sure that the records you see are actually held at the office and available for copying.

The records at FRC are held in indices covering years by quarters. Once you have located an ancestor and the GRO reference, you can order a copy of a birth, marriage or death certificate from the office and it will be posted to you.

VITAL STATISTICS
Here is the information on the certificates:

Births

- Name and sex of child
- Date and place of birth
- Name and surname of father
- Name and maiden name of mother
- Rank or profession of father.

Marriages

- Names and surnames of bride and groom
- When and where married
- Religous denomination
- Ages of bride and groom
- Rank or profession of bride and groom
- Residence at time of marriage
- Names of fathers of bride and groom
- Fathers' rank or profession.

Deaths

- Name and sex of deceased
- Date and place of death
- Age at death
- Rank or profession
- Cause of death
- Name, relationship and residence of informant.

You can also order certificates from the GRO main office at Southport by email, post and fax. This is the National Statistics Office, comprising the three GROs for England & Wales, Scotland and Northern Ireland respectively. The website is www.statistics.gov.uk, from which you can download an application form for a certificate.

Approximation

You don't need the GRO reference if you order from Southport, but the charge is less if you do. So it is possible to do searching by post rather than visit offices. Costs and other details are on the site. The certificates will give information such as parents, place and occupation so you will have reliable data to advance your search. You can, however, gather a lot of information from the indices by approximating dates. Many families lived in the same parish for generations so this will help validate a hit, especially in the case of an uncommon name. However, these are heavy index ledgers with four quarters to trawl for each year of your approximation range. So, whilst dealing just with indices it may make more sense first to do some online searching as discussed in Chapter 2, unless you particularly need the exercise.

Validation

When you combine marriage, death and children information with a birth you will add a lot to the validity of what you find even though you have not seen a copy of an original record. Bear in mind that the volume of names grows exponentially if you are searching full 'trees' rather than a single, direct line of a dozen or so generations, so it can be expensive to obtain copies of certificates. As I suggested earlier, you may wish to restrict copies to your direct line – your great, great, great etc. grandfathers – or to cases where there is uncertainty that will be cleared up by reference to the additional information on the certificate. It's up to you. It is nice to see a copy of actual certificates – this is what starts to bring your ancestors to life. Your great, great, great etc. grandfather's occupation may be of interest, for instance, and may lead you to more information about his life. Also remember that by locating addresses you have a basis for accessing census records.

The FRC is not the only place holding indices and providing copies of vital records. If you know the district in which the event happened you can apply to the local record office, and you may wish to consult microfiches of baptisms and burials on the same visit. You can find a list of registration districts, and the addresses of local offices that maintain the vital records, from which you can order copies, on the GENUKI web site.

www.freeband.org is a collaborative effort to place copies of birth, marriage and death indexes online. It is worth a visit although incomplete.

CENSUS RETURNS

With the exception of 1941 during the second world war, censuses have been taken every 10 years from 1801. The 1841 census was the first to contain details of the people in each dwelling, rather than just a head count, so that is the date from which they become useful to genealogists. They are released for public access only after 100 years so the 1901 census is now available, and – a major landmark for family historians – will go online with a name index. Check the PRO website. The only other census fully indexed at the time of writing is that for 1881, and the 1851 census is following along rapidly and is completed for some counties. Census returns are an enormous help in tracing ancestors, especially those from 1851 which include the age and place of birth of each family member, which helps you to track backwards a generation. The information on most census returns will include:

- Name
- Marital Status
- Age
- Occupation
- Birthplace.

Various counties have also been indexed for different decennial dates and you can get information about these from the respective local FH society. Contact the society in the area your searches are focused on to get up to date information of what is available. You can usually save time and effort by accessing an index in the first instance so it is as well to check what is available as soon as you locate where your ancestors lived. For Scotland, check www.scotsorigin.net for available census indexes and images.

Indexing and online access is advancing apace so a current internet search, say on GENUKI, is much more useful than the most recently published book for this purpose.

EXPLORING THE CATALOGUE

Appendix 1 shows the online summary catalogue of records at the PRO. Go to 'Catalogues' then 'PROCAT' online catalogue which contains details of over nine million files, organised by 'creating department'. You can search these to identify the PRO reference of documents you wish to consult, then order them or request copies. Choose 'Information Leaflets', then 'Information Leaflets for Researchers' and you will get the detailed records catalogue.

You can explore this for potential sources of information on your ancestors, or if you want to follow up a lead relating to a certain kind of record. These are not just summary headings but each is hypertexed to more detailed web pages that give you background information about the records and specific information about locating them. The following is the A section only:

Admiralty Charts (Maps)
Agricultural Statistics, from 1866 onwards: Parish Summaries
American and West Indian Colonies before 1782
American Revolution
Anglo-Jewish History: Sources in the PRO, 18th–20th Centuries
Apprenticeship Records as Sources for Genealogy
Architectural Drawings in the PRO
Assizes (English), 1656–1971: Key to Series for Civil Trials
Assizes (English), Key for Criminal Trials, 1559–1971
Assizes (Welsh), 1831–1971: Key to Classes for Criminal and Civil Trials
Assizes: Criminal Trials
Auxiliary Army Force: Volunteers Yeomanry, Territorials & Home Guard 1769–1945.

We can use this short section to illustrate how you can make your way around the catalogue, learning as you go. The item 'Apprenticeship Records as Source for Genealogy', for instance, looks like this:

Apprenticeship Records as Source for Genealogy

Domestic Records Information 80

1. Introduction

The Statute of Apprentices in 1563 forbade anyone to enter a trade who had not served an apprenticeship. Whilst the full rigour of this statute was modified by subsequent Acts of Parliament and by legal judgements, it remained on the statute book until 1814.

Until the Statute 8 Anne c.5 (1710) made stamp duty payable on indentures of apprenticeship, no central register of apprentices was kept in England

and Wales, and evidence of apprenticeship must therefore be sought locally, in the surviving papers of firms, parishes, charities and individuals. (See, for example, W B Stephens, *Sources of English Local History* (1981).

2. Apprenticeship Books, 1710–1811 – IR 1

For the years 1710 to 1811 the Commissioners of Stamps kept registers of the money they received from the duty of indentures. These now form the Apprenticeship Books (IR 1) at the Public Record Office. Duty was payable by the master at the rate of 6d for every £1 under £50 which he received for taking on the apprentice, and 1s for every £1 above that sum. The deadline for payment was one year after the expiry of the indenture; it may therefore be necessary to search the records of several years' payments in order to find a particular entry, even when the date of the indenture is known.

The Apprenticeship Books record the names, addresses and trades of the masters, the names of the apprentices and dates of their indentures. Until 1752 the names of apprentices' parents are given, but after that year rarely. Microfiche copies of indices of masters', and of apprentices' names, both from 1710 to 1774 will be found in the Microfilm Reading Room; this replaces and extends former record series IR 17 which has now been destroyed. These are copies of those created by the Society of Genealogists, and a further set of copies are in the Guildhall Library, London.

Where the stamp duty was paid in London, entries will be found in the 'City' registers in this series; where it was paid elsewhere, entries will be found in the 'County' registers.

A typical entry in the fiche index to apprentices will look like this:

41/27   This is the piece number in IR1 and the folio:
film IR 1/41 look at folio 27

1710   This is the year indentures were registered:
up to 1 year after the end of the apprenticeship, which might be for up to 7 years

Ferrand   This is the Surname of apprentice:
spelling variants may be grouped together

Rob   This is the Forename of the apprentice

Sam of Rotherham, Yks, Clk   This is the parent's or guardian's name (rare after 1752)
son of is always omitted
Surname is omitted if the same as the apprentice's
Forenames are abbreviated
Occupations are abbreviated – see list at the beginning of index fiche
cit (for citizen) implies Freedom of the city of London and membership of a livery company

to Jn Marsden of Liverpool marin   This is the Master's name:
Forenames are abbreviated
Occupations are abbreviated –
see list at the beginning of each index volume
cit (for citizen) implies freedom of the city of London and membership of a livery company

£25   This is the Value of agreement (notional)

The full entry in the Apprenticeship Book (IR 1/41 folio 27) reads:

John Marsden of Liverpool, mariner took as apprentice Robt, son of Sam Ferrand of the parish of Rotherham in the county of York., clerk, by Common Indenture and Counterpart, dated 29 September [1710] for 6 years from that date, for under £25. Collector was Ed: Vaudrey at Warrington, Lancaster; duty payable 12/6. Registered: 15 December 1710.

3. Apprenticeships not Recorded in the Apprenticeship Books

Formal indentures involved some trouble and expense. By the eighteenth century apprenticeships were often undertaken without any formal indenture, especially in common trades such as weaving. In many trades it was expected that men would bring up their sons or nephews to the trade. Further, it was ruled that the Statute if Apprentices did not extend to trades which did not exist when it was passed in 1563; this excluded many eighteenth-century industries, most notably the cotton industry. In many areas the Statute was not enforced, and in the Yorkshire woollen industry formal apprenticeships hardly existed by the end of the eighteenth century.

A large proportion of those who were formally indentured were taken on by masters at the expense of the parish or a public charity. These indentures were exempt from stamp duty (8 Anne c.5) and the apprentices are thus not included in the registers. In such cases, local or charity records, if they survive, are likely to be the only source of information.

4. Some Other Apprenticeship Records in the PRO

Apprenticeship is touched on in the records of a number of other departments. The following notes indicate some of the records which yield names of individual apprentices.

◆ **War Office:**

The Alphabetical Guide to War Office and other Materials (PRO Lists and Indices, LIII) gives several references, particularly to letters and Law Officers' Opinions on the recurrent controversy of the eighteenth and early nineteenth centuries whether apprentices might enlist in the army or be recruited again against their masters' wishes. A list survives of recruits surrendered for this reason between 1806 and 1835 (<u>WO 25/2962</u>).

◆ **Admiralty:**

Correspondence on the subject of Apprentices will be found by means of the Digest and Indices (<u>ADM 12</u>), under headings such as 'Boys' (code 13) and 'Apprentices in Dockyards' (code 41.16). References from this source must be keyed up with the lists of correspondence of the Admiralty (<u>ADM 1</u>) and Navy Board (<u>ADM 106</u>). The Miscellaneous Registers of Greenwich Hospital include apprenticeship registers (<u>ADM 73/421</u>, <u>ADM 73/448</u>). Marks and results of examinations for dockyard and artificer apprentices from 1876 will be found among the records of the Civil Service Commission (<u>CSC 10</u>).

◆ **Registrar General Of Shipping And Seamen:**

Under the Merchant Seamen Act of 1823, ships of over 80 tons had to carry apprentices, whose names were to be enrolled with local customs officials. Under the Merchant Seamen Act of 1835 registration of apprentices in London was to be by the Registrar General, to whom also returns of regional registration (still made by local customs officials) were to be submitted quarterly. Compulsory apprenticeship was abolished in 1849, but registers were still maintaned of those who were apprenticed after that date. Indices of Apprentices registered in the merchant service between 1824 and 1953 will be found in the series <u>BT 150</u>, where the earlier volumes give the apprentice's name, age, the date and terms of his indenture, and the name of his master. Later volumes (<u>BT 150/15</u> et seq.) include also the port where he signed on and the name of the ship. Samples of the original indentures, including some for fishing vessels, will be found in <u>BT 151</u> and <u>BT 152</u>.

◆　**Board Of Trade:**

The Indices to Papers retained (BT 19) include references to Apprenticeship, which may be keyed up with the correspondence of the various departments of the Board as explained in the Guide on the Research Enquiries Room shelves.

◆　**Poor Law Union Papers:**

The Index of Subjects (MH 15) includes mention of Apprenticeship, mainly to questions of policy and precedent. The references there given may, in some cases, be keyed up with the papers of the individual Poor Law Unions in MH 12, which may yield further records not mentioned in the Index.

You will see that the leaflet provides all the information you are likely to need about the nature of the records, including how the microfiche index appears.

I have included another example to illustrate the value of these information leaflets. Choose 'Assizes: Criminal Trials' near the bottom of the As. Notice the list of Latin abbreviations which you can use for reference purposes or as a handy self-tutor.

Assizes: Criminal Trials

Legal Records Information 13

1. Introduction

The assizes were held twice each year from the 13th Century to 1971 in each county, grouped into a number of circuits. In 1971 they were abolished (in 1956 for Liverpool and Manchester) and replaced by the crown courts.

2. Early Assize Records

From the 13th century, judges and senior lawyers were commissioned as justices to ride off and hold the king's courts. A pair of judges would cover a circuit, each circuit covering a group of counties. (London, Middlesex and the palatinates were not included). Originally they mainly tried property disputes, but they came to try criminal cases also, including those sent out for trial from the central courts to assizes under the *nisi prius* system. Their records are in JUST 1–JUST 4. From 1482 to 1559 there is a gap in the surviving records of the assizes, although quite a lot can be discovered from the indictments in KB 9 returned from lower courts, often via the assizes, into King's Bench, and a considerable number of letters from the assize judges, reporting back to the centre on the political condition of the country, start to survive (in SP 1), and after throughout the State Papers, Domestic.

3. Assize Records, 1559–1971

By 1559, from when the records of the Home Circuit only start to survive in quantity, the assize judges mainly dealt with the more serious criminal offences not normally handled by the local courts of Quarter Sessions. Offences dealt with range from homicide, infanticide, theft (stolen goods were often under-valued as worth less than 12d to avoid making it a capital offence), highway robbery, rape, assault, coining, forgery and witchcraft, to trespass, vagrancy and recusancy.

Before 1733 most Assize records are in Latin. They do not normally give the age of the accused or details of family. Aliases were common, and occupations and place of abode are not trustworthy. J S Cockburn's *A History of English Assizes, 1558–1714* (1972) and his *Calendars of Assize Records* for the Home Circuit (Essex, Herts, Kent, Surrey and Sussex) for 1558–1625, continued to 1684. For Kent, these are an invaluable guide to assize records. The introductory volume is particularly valuable in pointing out the pitfalls in taking the records at face value. See also L Knafla, *Kent at Law, 1602* (1994). *Criminal Ancestors* by D T Hawkings (1992) also covers assizes and related records.

4. Finding Out Where a Trial Took Place

The assize records are not indexed by personal name: instead, they are arranged by assize circuit, and then by record type. To find a particular case, you must know the name of the accused; the county or circuit where he/she was tried and the approximate date of the trial. For the nineteenth century, if you do not know where or when the accused was tried, you can look at the Criminal Registers, for England and Wales 1805–1892 in HO 27. These list those charged with indictable offences, giving place of trial, verdict and sentence. From 1868 (subject to 75–100 year closure), there are also the Calendars of prisoners tried at assizes and quarter sessions in HO 140.

Once you have a reference to a date and place of trial, check in English Assizes: Key to Records of Criminal Trials, or Welsh Assizes, 1831–1971: Key to Classes for Criminal and Civil Trials under the county you are interested in, to find out what records survive. Survival of assize records is patchy, as the clerks of assize, whe kept them, tended to destroy them when their bulk became too much. Few counties other than those in the North have surviving depositions before the 19th century and a few Midland Circuit records survive before 1818. If a suitable record exists for the year and place in question, go to the class list of the class indicated.

5. Where to Start in the Assize Records

The best place to begin a search in the assize records themselves is with the Crown Minute Book, Gaol Book or Agenda Book if one survives – these list the accused and summarize cases heard, or about to be heard, often noting the plea, verdict and sentence. There may be a separate series of minute books for offences, such as the failure of local communities to keep local roads and bridges in a good state of repair. The indictments are the formal statement of the charge against the accused, usually annotated with plea, verdict and sentence and filed in large unwieldy bundles together with other miscellaneous records such as jury panels, coroner's inquests, commissions and presentments of non-criminal offences. Further information about indictments is given in the series description to ASSI 5. Depositions and Examinations can be full of personal details but have mostly not survived – there is a good series from 1613 on in ASSI 45 which have been listed in detail to 1800 and indexed by type of offence.

Transcripts of proceedings or shorthand notes of what was actually said in court do not normally survive with the records held here, although contemporary newspapers or pamphlets often reported local cases in much detail. Local newspapers may be consulted at the British Library's Newspaper Library at Colindale or sometimes at the apporopriate local county record office or library.

6. No Surviving Assize Records?

If no records appear to have survived for your county, for 1714–1832 you should look at the incomplete series of sheriffs' assize vouchers in E 389/241–257. They can include lists of prisoners tried or transported, accounts for maintenence in prison or carrying out an execution. For example, for Northampton, no assize records survive for 1776, but E 389/245/8 lists the names, offences and verdicts of those tried at Northampton at the Lent Assizes of 1776. Copies of indictments removed to the Court of King's Bench by writs of *certiorari* and returns in KB 9 of those granted benefit of clergy (before 1660) can also help to fill gaps.

7. Latin Abbreviations (Still Used After 1733)

ca null	*catalla nulla*	no goods/chattels to forfeit
cog ind	*cognovit indictamentum*	confessed to the indictment
cul	*Culpabilis*	Guilty
ign	*Ignoramus*	we do not know i.e. no case to answer
non cul nec re	*non culpabilis nec retraxit*	not guilty and did not flee
po se	*ponit se super patrium*	puts himself on the country, i.e. opts for jury trial and pleads not guilty
sus	*Suspendatur*	let him be hanged

8. London and Middlesex

London and Middlesex sessions before 1834 were held before the lord mayor – records relating to the City are now in the Corporation of London Record Office and those for the rest of London and Middlesex are with the London Metropolitan Archives. After 1834, the Central Criminal Court acted as the assize for London, Middlesex and parts of Essex, Kent and Surrey – see Old Bailey and the Central Criminal Court : Criminal Trials. There are printed proceedings for London and Middlesex cases 1801–1834 in PCOM 1 and for Central Criminal Court cases in CRIM 10 (1834–1912) and some shorthand notes in cases where the Director of Public Prosecutions or Treasury Solicitor had an interest in DPP 4 (after 1846) and TS 36 (unlisted) and in cases that were referred to the Court of Criminal Appeal in J 82 (after 1945).

9. Bristol, Wales, Chester, Durham and Lancaster

Bristol sessions records before 1832 are held by Bristol Record Office. Wales came under the Court of Great Sessions, 1543–1830, the records of which are held by the National Library of Wales, Aberystwyth, Dyfed SY23 3BU. From 1830, the Welsh records are held here. Chester, Durham and Lancaster were palatinates with their own assize jurisdiction until 1830 for Chester and 1876 for Durham and Lancaster.

The underlined items are hypertext that take you to another source type of leaflet, or more detailed information.

Searching and downloading

You can do a word search of all nine million records and order or download a record image. Choose 'Research' then 'How to See the Records' then 'PRO-Online'. There is a small charge for digital images of wills and maps but other images are free. So you can have a ball. You can download Shakespeare's last will and testament free to try out the system.

Check on 'Technical Information' for full directions about using PRO-Online.

The above is an introduction to accessing public records and illustrates the enormous range of record types and sources. Having conducted online surname searches as we described in Chapter 2, you can now locate these at the PRO or relevant county record office and obtain copies of certificates. You can also start exploring the catalogue and printing out leaflets on any topics you want to pursue. Chapter 8 gives more examples of what you can search in order to get to know ancestors who are only names and dates.

FIGURE 10 Beginning of Shakespeare's will

7

Interpreting Old Records

If you haven't come across records that are difficult to read, whether in terms of the language, spelling or just the antiquity and condition of the document, it probably means you haven't tracked very far back and have been less than successful in your endeavours. Or maybe you have a working knowledge of Latin, Old English and palaeography. For most readers, tracing ancestors to the sixteenth century through parish records will be a feasible objective, but the contemporary will and testament of William Shakespeare we have just seen illustrates the problems of comprehending old documents, let alone accurate transcription as we discussed in Chapter 4.

Unintelligibility, to some degree or other – especially when you move on from the more common, vital records – is at the core of the family history process. The oldest records are more or less a different language. Even handwriting as we know it is a relative innovation. The difficulty of understanding old records affects people differently. In one case it is a challenge, providing endless pleasure; in another case it brings a summary end to family history aspirations. I have therefore included sections in the chapter addressing our attitude and approach, as well as some of the mechanics and conventions with which we need to be familiar.

Fortunately, the 'work backwards' rule we met at the start means that this aspect of family history doesn't confront you suddenly. In practice you will gradually meet quaint or ambiguous records that you can interpret and transcribe quite easily and add to your personal skill and knowledge database one step at a time.

In one respect this gradual, or 'need to know' basis is the only feasible way to approach old records, language and palaeography as there is so much variety. These variations in recording are more or less unlimited, as are the specialised subjects that family history draws upon, and the depth of skill to which you can aspire. A working knowledge of Latin or Old English and the development of old handwriting are just the obvious ones. Family history covers every aspect of social and economic history, and that is part of the fascinating package of getting to know your ancestors.

KNOWING WHAT'S IMPORTANT

Thankfully old records can be a perfectly manageable challenge for the average family historian. The thanks go to the ubiquitous 80–20 rule which says something like we use 80 per cent of our time and effort producing 20 per cent of what we want, or outputs, and vice versa. Applied to genealogy, reasonable knowledge and skill in 20 per cent of 'inputs' (spelling, language, transcription etc. – the *main* factors) will cover perhaps 80 per cent of what we are after – our aims, 'outputs' and what we reveal of our ancestors.

By the same token, beyond that level of knowledge and expertise, additional knowledge and skill would probably not make a proportionate impact on your results. The relationship reverses and 80 per cent of your effort produces just 20 per cent of the results you want. Or, according to another ubiquitous rule, you get diminishing returns for your time and effort. Even full time professionals cannot afford to go to the nth degree in their research, and they too, knowingly or unknowingly, apply this 'what is important' philosophy. The good news is that many thousands of family historians produce remarkable results as amateurs, and enthusiasm makes up a lot for lack of professional training. An important part of this core know-how is understanding old records.

Mistakes galore

We can also be thankful that what is important has long since been identified by generations of genealogists who learned the hard way – by making mistakes galore and putting disproportionate effort into relatively fruitless activities. For example, the handful of 'rules' for budding family historians in the 'Getting Started' chapter are a small selection of the rules promulgated over the years, yet they will take care of most of the pitfalls and tears that otherwise we would face. Put another way, stick to a few common sense guidelines and you will have a sporting chance of success. When it comes to old records – or any aspect of your family history interests – a few carefully chosen bits of knowledge and core researching skills will suffice for most people most of the time. Mistakes are inevitable, but it is better to learn from one rather than six.

Critical content

Another general 'what's important' point arises as a variation of the above rules. Not every word or event has equal importance to your overall research. Names, for example, have high priority, along with places and dates as they form a foundation for later research. You should therefore apply any rules rigorously, first to certain kinds of documents (such as parish vital records as compared with personal letters or the minutia of a land transfer) and then to the critical content (or data fields) within those documents. In short, keep the forest as well as the trees in mind and apply common sense. Fortunately, vital data can usually be corroborated from other records: but we need first to recognise it as vital.

Trees and forest

A 'trees and forest', or 'detail and big picture' approach applies across the board. There are some things that a detailed word by word study will not reveal, such as the context and comparisons in other parts of a document. Likewise, a fast skim read will miss important detail. This calls for a two-level approach in which you apply quite different thinking style or skills. A word by word blind 'translation' will probably suffice for most of the text, leaving unknown or doubtful words and phrases for later. These then become more obvious in their context on a 'big picture', 'common sense' reading. The point is that a two-level method is more productive in the long run as sometimes we *never* see the forest for the trees, however much effort we apply. Most of us get bogged down by a 21st century official document so we need to make a few allowances for records before the nineteenth century.

A fast read has other advantages, such as when you first need to determine whether a document is relevant in the first place, or is likely to contain the information you are seeking. Conversely, a slow read may throw up clues and insights that you had not set out to address, yet may open important new lines of enquiry that would have been missed by any less thorough method. There's art and science combined, and some serendipity.

Secretary hand

Much of the difficulty in reading old documents relates simply to the personal style of the handwriting, complete with flourishes and idiosyncratic embellishments. Some types of handwriting were not taught at school, but by notaries and other professionals to their clerks or students. For example the 'secretary hand', the 'italic hand', and the 'court hand' all had distinctive forms of character and abbreviations. All this is on top of the differences as taught by different teachers, and of course the individual's own style. You may recall from historical novels that a man's and woman's 'hand' were apparently easily distinguishable. Most of the basic information in this chapter applies to any 'hand'.

HAVING THE RIGHT ATTITUDE

Besides keeping things in perspective it helps to have the right attitude. This kind of research can easily get under your skin. Understand that the countless scribes of yesteryear did not set out to make life either easy or hard for future generations of genealogists. They just did their jobs. And the records they made fulfilled their own requirements, which were not only nothing to do with future family history, but also varied from record to record and place to place.

Offending scribes

There is method in this pragmatic approach. By understanding the purpose of the document and documenter, interpretation becomes so much easier and even 'common sense' – something, once shown, we can all live with. For example, the desire to produce an impressive looking document – when even basic literacy was impressive – might easily account for those hyperbolic squiggles and meaningless prose. Likewise, the desire to produce documents unintelligible to all but one specialised profession (such as the law) in order to maintain a semblance of mystique and scarcity value is not, in fact, so ancient. So don't take anything personally, least of all when the offending scribe has been long since dead.

Hand-carved

Remember also that records were made by individuals, with their own ideas, feelings, talents and intentions. They even had their own grammar and spelling. In an age of universal illiteracy there was not much accountability nor standards to apply. Why shouldn't a clerk spell a name three different ways in the course of a single document if its owner couldn't spell at all, and it made no difference to the purpose of the record or the efficiency of the system it supported? Thus old documents can be like a hand-carved ornament, as unique as the human documenter and documented.

COMPARISON OF ARCHIVES

Much of the methodology of understanding archives boils down to comparison. For example, comparing unknown words and characters with known ones in the same document. Depending on the size of the document, start from the same page, then work forwards and backwards page by page in turn – you may not have to check far for a given word, and familiarity will help with other queries. The job is much easier if you know the context and what is probably being communicated or recorded. Thus by finding a difficult word or character whose meaning is clear, you can better understand it in a less obvious context. A few very common words together account for most letters of the alphabet so you can soon determine how the writer penned them and used them in the words you cannot understand.

Detection and deciphering

For example, many letters of the alphabet occur in the combined months of the year, and dates appear in most kinds of record, so you can refer specifically to them for a handy character deciphering code. Similarly, some phrases like 'in the parish of' recur. Just a few such phrases will unlock mystery characters, and there are scores of legal terms applying to different kinds of document. Add the months of the year and very common words, including first names, and you have keys to what may appear like a foreign language.

The longer the overall document, the more chance there is of getting your solutions by comparison within the document. In the case of a parish register, the same priest or clerk would typically make entries over a period of years, so you have lots of material to work on. Be ready to move around the microfiche! In the case of a shorter, stand alone document, you can of course refer to other documents written by the same person (during the same date period in the same office) to interpret personal handwriting style or spelling. You are unlikely to be confronted with the Dead Sea scrolls and most difficulties are amenable to common-sense comparison.

Once you have deduced the writer's personal alphabet, plus recurring idiosyncrasies, you can decode it routinely. If it is a particularly problematic record it makes sense to build up an 'alphabet' *first* from common or well-understood words before you start getting down to the overall meaning, thus saving a lot of frustration and, in the long run, time and effort.

Abbreviation

The same detective work applies to abbreviations, although in most cases you can swot up on common abbreviations or refer to a dictionary of archival abbreviations, and you have a glossary at the end of the book. By locating the same abbreviation in different parts of the document or in other documents you can usually work out its meaning, just as with words. Some common abbreviations are:

- **sd** for said
- **do** for ditto
- **chh** for church
- **decd** for deceased
- **rect** for receipt.

Double letters may be written as single letters with a line or 'tilde' above the letter (as above the n in the Spanish señor). Christian name abbreviations usually consisted of the first two, three or four letter plus the last letter, as in Saml or Thos. Abbreviation of names and common words usually show the last letter raised.

The worst thing is to make pot guesses, especially with abbreviated names, where there is at best room for ambiguity. Family history starts with positive identity. Far better to record exactly what you see and make the cynical assumptions we listed in the Getting Started and Transcription chapters. Do your detective work when you don't have the time pressure of transcription at a public record office and when you need to focus on routine recording rather than analysis.

CONVENTIONS AND CAVEATS

Some conventions were very common and are useful to bear in mind. Likewise, true to the 80–20 rule, many apparent irregularities are easily explained, or at least can be borne in mind and thus make an old document more friendly.

Characters

Differences from what we are familiar with extend to overall language and style, and the physical characteristics of the document, but we can start at the level of individual characters:

- In the case of double ss, the first s in the pair looked like a lower case f.
- Some capital letters looked the same: I and J; L and S; T, M and N; T and F; U and V. You may have noticed Latin inscriptions where the I is a modern day J and the V is a modern day U, or old museum stone entrance inscription as MVSEVM (hence double U is double V – W).
- Rounded lower case characters might appear the same, such as a, o and u, as the a and o might be left open at the top and the u almost closed.

- Some of the letters were often wrong because of the closeness of the sounds. These include V and B, V and W, D and T, B and P, F and P, F and V, S and X, G and K, W and R and are taken account of in the Soundex phonetic system.

- Double letters in a name could become single and vice versa.

- The vowels I, IE, EY and Y were often interchanged, and the same applied to O and OE, A and AY. E or S at the end of the word might be randomly added or omitted.

- Sometimes vowels were completely missing from the middle of a name leaving a string of consonants, like some modern forms of shorthand.

- A character may differ depending on where it lies in a word (such as at the end) or which character it precedes or follows.

Capitalisation

Further differences occur in the use of capital letters. To start with, there was not the consistency that we now apply, such as applying capitals to proper names and at the beginnning of a sentence. Words in the middle of a sentence might be capitalised for no apparent reason and a sentence might start with a lower case letter, all with impunity. However, mid-sentence capitalisation was usually for simple emphasis, such as Born, Baptised or Married, which will be apparent from the context if not the word itself.

Punctuation

Caveats that apply to capitalisation apply equally to punctuation generally. For example:

- Neither the presence nor the absence of a full stop indicates with any certainty the end of a sentence.
- Commas, colons and semicolons were used randomly for all practical purposes of family history research. A colon, for example, might indicate an abbreviation rather then an ensuing list or statement.
- A dash/hyphen or equal sign might indicate the end of a line or an abbreviation.
- A double hyphen similar to a modern equal sign was also used to denote part of a word carried to the next line, such as is now commonly hyphenated.
- That double hyphen might then be repeated on the new line, or new page – plus maybe the 'carried over' word itself – to show the contin=
  =uation of the text.

The good news is that individual recorders, being creatures of habit, were fairly consistent, mostly maintaining the same punctuation conventions (if not spelling) throughout. So comparisons within a document or the product of the same writer are likely to be at least as fruitful as the spelling comparisons we have already referred to. Also encouraging is the fact that with practice you will soon develop the necessary skill, and there will be less mystique to obscure recording conventions. Before long the researcher begins to look forward to finding practices not hitherto confronted, and sees it as a challenge rather than a chore. It is fair to say that, even with all the basic rules and forewarning, these key skills only come with practice. Like riding a bike or swimming, there is only so far you can go without having a go.

Meaning

An underrated problem is understanding the meaning of the same words that were used to mean something different in the historical period in question. This is rather like when the same word has a different meaning in the US from in the UK, and is far more prone to errors than when the word itself differs, such as sidewalk and pavement. In family history we have another dimension to cope with as meanings evolve over time as well as varying geographically.

In family history research, understandably, many cases involve family relationships. Here are some examples:

◆ The terms 'niece' and 'nephew' stem from Latin words that meant respectively granddaughter and grandson, so you may find them used in that way.

◆ The terms brother and sister are not always used in the literal sense we are familiar with. Readers of classical novels will know that sisters-in-law and brothers-in-law were welcomed into a family as 'sisters' and 'brothers', so there was no distinction (in the description) between a blood relationship and one by marriage. 'Brother' and 'sister' were also terms used in churches and societies, as they sometimes still are.

◆ 'Good brother' and 'good sister', on the other hand, referred to brother-in-law and sister-in-law respectively, and had nothing to do with the moral character of the person. 'Good son' and 'good daughter' might similarly refer to a son-in-law and daughter-in-law.

◆ Just to confuse matters completely, the term in-law might refer either to the relationship by marriage as we use the term today or a step relationship as we understand the term.

- The term 'infant' did not necessarily mean a baby or even a child, but a person below the legal age of majority, as we use the term 'minor'.
- The terms 'junior' and 'senior' that we use in a father–son relationship were once used more liberally. They might refer to an uncle or nephew, for example, or two people of the same name who were not related.

If you follow the rules we covered at the beginning, these anomalies should not present much difficulty. They usually occur in other than vital records, from which we confirm or corroborate rather than establish relationships, or sources that add historical interest. By knowing of them in advance, it just means that you will not spend unnecessary time on sorting out an apparent anomaly in your research. The general rule of corroborating relationships from as many sources as possible (birth, death, marriages, census, wills etc.) is the best safeguard against historical irregularities that were not used *consistently* irregularly in any case. Don't take anything at face value.

Names and the invention of spelling

People's names and place names are another example of the absence of standardisation. There are great variations in early documents, but this doesn't mean the recorders were any more prone to error than we are today. Spelling wasn't 'invented' until 1755, in the sense of spelling rules. In that year Samuel Johnson published the first Dictionary of the English Language, but for long after that date spelling was not standardised. Most people couldn't read or write anyway, and those who could, such as priests and clerks, did so at very different standards, and were unlikely to be corrected anyway as spelling was not important. As we have seen, names and any other words might change several times in the same document. Hence the variations we tend to find reflect pronunciation or phonetics more than anything. This introduces the effects of dialects as well as the problems of oral communication that apply as much today when talking on the telephone and – for many people – having to repeatedly spell out your name.

A principle in genealogy is to work on name sounds rather than exact spellings. The tendency should be to use as many personal name variations in your research as may exist rather than assume there is something special about the current version of your surname and that anything different cannot be part of your pedigree.

Name spelling has special significance in genealogy, of course, and is not confined to old documents. It may result in missing chunks of collected data gathered under another version of the name. Indices such as the IGI that automatically include Soundex variations are very helpful, especially as the index is often the first port of call.

On top of all these fairly understandable variations are the same sort of 'typos' that appear today whether in handwriting or, especially, emails, and mainly comprising juxtaposed letters, or randomly appearing or disappearing letters.

Name change

Deliberate name changes are another factor affecting old records. There was no more need to stick to the same name centuries ago as there is today. We are free to change our names as we like, and this was common practice in certain situations, such as when people emigrated from one country to another, moved to another town, or changed their work. Nowadays the main constraint on name changing is the nuisance value as we all have so many records held in our name. (Email address changing is an international pastime). Obviously the problem gets bigger as we search progressively further back beyond the introduction of civil B, D and M registration and before common literacy.

Place name changes

Changes have also occurred in place names, with substantial county changes, for example, in the 20th century. The reasons and range vary as with people's names, but in addition place names may change because of widespread boundary changes, such as affected the English counties in 1974. Towns and parishes landed up in different counties, some counties disappeared and others were created.

Following boundary changes the records sometimes stay in the old location rather than a new centre of administration so it can easily throw you off a trail if you do not allow for the possibility. Gazetteers record place names and changes and you can do place searches just as with surnames on some of the main FH websites. Maps at the dates of important changes are a helpful resource if place takes on an important aspect of your work. The FamilySearch website has UK maps pre- and post- the 1974 local government reorganisation, for instance, which you can download or copy (for your own use). Once you have established the main place or places where your ancestors came from you can get to know the place history as a one-off project.

This range of topics concerning old records is par for the course in family history and is an essential part of an activity that relies so much on old, original documents. Approached in the right frame of mind, it is all part of the fun and fascination.

When faced with problems bear in mind the wealth of experience represented around the world through family history societies, mailing lists, newsgroups and professional organisations. Maybe no one has attempted to track down your particular ancestors, but it is almost certain that the sort of records you will consult and the kinds of problems you encounter will not be new to the world of genealogy. Take full advantage of these resources, covered mainly in Chapters 3 and 5, which are growing all the time.

Ordinary world wide web browser searches under the headings of punctuation, spelling, palaeography etc. will also reap rewards, whether to gain more general knowledge or to help answer specific queries. Or do a thorough job and treat yourself to a course in palaeography or secretary handwriting – whatever takes your interest and helps to advance your family history research. Check out local courses through FH societies or further education institutes (usually more general or introductory), the organisations in Chapter 5, or do a search of the web on your favourite browser.

MEDIAEVAL PUBLIC RECORDS

The real challenges for family historians lie before the introduction of parish registers in 1538. Before that date births, marriages and deaths were not officially recorded although notes may have been kept by priests. However, several kinds of records started well before that date. In general they contain information about the wealthier members of society. Information about the masses of ordinary people are very sparse, and occur in records such as land transfers and trials.

The challenges go beyond scarcity, however. Older records are more difficult to read, being usually in a highly abbreviated form of Latin. Latin was used in formal records until 1733 and English started to become more common in the late fifteenth century. The use of surnames was not general until about 1300, and there was no consistency of spelling. We saw in Chapter 2 that surnames were not always passed from generation to generation, and different names could be used in different contexts.

Fortunately for today's family historians, many of the mediaeval records have been published and these form the basis for much research into this period. Most of these published records can be seen at the PRO library, or in the Map and Large Document Room (more on PRO records in Chapter 8). You can get general help, but that does not include translation. So depending on your needs, and the extent to which you want to learn skills yourself, you may want to hire a specialist for particular research. You will need to get prepared, of course, with specific questions. Sources are basically searched either by name or place, because of the nature of the record or the way it has been indexed, so the information you already have may dictate where you start looking. Remember also that family history can be found in any kinds of document, not just those which we think of as genealogical. Hence, a standard web-wide rather than FH site search – perhaps through a multi-browser like Copernic, or several popular search engines – might produce help and information that even Cyndi's List and the PRO did not offer. Finally, by following the 'work backwards' rule, by the time you reach the oldest records you will have gained plenty of hard experience, plus knowledge of where to get help.

8

Getting to Know Your Ancestors

Successful family historians produce more than hierarchies of names and dates, however far back into antiquity they reach. They capture unique insights into real people and the environment in which they lived. Chapters 2 and 6 focused mainly on vital (B, D and M) public records. In addition to these, the PRO and local record offices contain a vast range of other public records that make family history the absorbing passion it is for so many. Chapter 3 was concerned with online internet resources, and this also showed the scope and variety of public records and where they are located. But your research will usually bring you physically back to the main record offices, and especially the PRO and the FRC in London and the record office in the county in which your tree originates. It is when you get close to original documents and the wealth of records beyond key life events, that you will start to get to know your ancestors as real people. In this chapter we will look further at a few main categories that provide these 'true stories' and help you with non-standard searches.

Your best preparation is by visiting each record office or library website and learning whatever you can from the printable leaflets, help guides and articles freely available.

From the main examples in this chapter you will get a flavour for what you will find, but inevitably in less detail, plus a few tips and information to boost your confidence as you extend your research. The space I have given does not reflect the relative volume or importance of a category of record. I have simply chosen interesting or representative bits of information, focusing rather on how you can get information and utilise all the resources under your own steam (and learn much faster in the process). Once you acquire the basic knowledge and 'how to' skills – by having a go – you need never get stuck, even on the less common kinds of research.

If you have no specific leads to follow, as you read this chapter you may fancy pursuing one or more specialised areas that had not occurred to you. You can download PRO leaflets covering most FH topics and recorded types. These are listed in Appendix 1 and I have referred to some of them below, adding some historical background to the records. You will then have enough information to explore deeper into a particular public record source.

You can generally search the records either by a person's name or their place of birth, so the many additional records you can access will depend partly on what information you already have. From the work you have done on vital records you will probably have a name, date of birth or baptism and parish, so that gives you access to records of many types. Given firm 'place' information, knowledge of the local industry, topography, traditions, crafts, economy, domestic conditions and general way of life will provide a backdrop to anyone who was born and raised there. This is often covered by published material, as well as manorial and other archives.

To help you get started, in the first part of the chapter I have given a pot pourri of examples of records indexed or listed by name and those indexed by place. This might suggest what you can investigate next, to make the best use of indices and the information you already have. Further information about the main categories of records themselves then forms the rest of the chapter.

NAME SEARCHES

Wills are a fruitful source of information when starting with a name, as they contain lots of family detail that offers new lines of enquiry and clues. The PRO has wills dating back to 1383. These are wills handled by the church court known as the Prerogative Court of Canterbury. These mainly comprise wealthy men, unmarried women and widows dying in the south of England and abroad. Inquisitions post mortem are another source of information, again for people of some social standing. Documents issued from or inspected by the Royal Chancery have mostly been published until the late 1500s. These relate primarily to those whose status involved direct dealings with central government, but they contain references to many other people as well. Registers of the King's (Privy) Council have also been published and indexed, so you can do a quick name search even if you think your chances of a hit are low. Although some mediaeval record types continue to the present, because only the earliest have been published this is an instance where the further back you research the easier it gets.

Large numbers of letters and papers survive relating to the government of the day, dating from the beginning of the 16th century and referred to as the State Papers, Domestic. These are well indexed, so it is worth a name check on a visit to the PRO. Don't forget to record what you have checked so that you can eliminate that source from future research. Similar papers exist for Scotland, Ireland and colonial and foreign affairs. Covering the economic life of the nation are various series of Calendars of Treasury Books and Papers, 1557–1704, also well indexed. Remember that lots of individual indices means lots of searches, so allow yourself plenty of time.

PLACE SEARCHES

Once you locate where your ancestors lived you can trace them through manorial records extending back to the Norman conquest. These records were kept on behalf of the lords of manors who were both landlords and local judicial and administrative authorities. So you will find records of land transactions, minor lawsuits and minor breaches of the peace. 'Rentals' and 'surveys' name tenants and describe individual holdings, so you can often trace a peasant's line back through centuries. Ministers' and receivers' accounts were also kept by officials responsible for the revenues of manors and other estates and these included the names of tenants. Manorial documents are mainly housed at CROs but you can find a large number at the PRO, mostly in respect of crown lands. You can also access the Manorial Documents Register at the National Register of Archives, the Royal Commission on Historical Manuscripts in London. From 'place' information you can also refer to Muster rolls that recorded the names of able-bodied men between the age of 16 and 60 liable for military service. Taxation records also cover rich and poor (but not the very poor who were exempt) alike. A wide range of taxation records is available, as well as exemption certificates for paupers. The poll tax returns of 1378 covering most male adults, often give occupations and the relationship between members of the household. The lists are by county, then by hundred or wapentake rather than parish or manor.

INHERITANCE RECORDS

Inheritance records comprise death duties, wills, administrations and disputes. A good place to start is the death duty registers and indices covering the period 1796 to 1858.

Death duties

Death duty records are not by date of death, but by date of probate or issue of the grant of administration. The indices will tell you where the will was proved (judged valid) or the administration issued (where there was no valid will). Not all wills and administrations appear in these indices, but it is worth starting here.

From 1796 death duties were payable on estates above a certain value, which has of course changed over the years. The scope of duty extended so that by 1857 there should be an entry for all estates worth over £20. The registers show what happened to a person's estate after death and what it was actually worth after debts and expenses. They may also include the date of death, information about beneficiaries, who were next of kin, relationship to the deceased and so on. Registers were annotated for up to 50 years so lots of additional information may appear regarding spouses, posthumous children, changes of address and such like.

The registers go up to 1903 when they stopped because of a change in Inland Revenue filing, the individual files from that date being destroyed after 30 years. So between 1796 and 1903 family historians can find information from these records not available elsewhere. Most of the records can be seen on microfilm at the PRO and FRC and you can get more information about actual archives from the websites, from downloadable leaflets, or by email or telephone.

See also the PRO leaflet *Death Duty Records from 1796.*

Wills

We have said that wills are a fruitful source of information, especially before civil registration of births, deaths and marriages was introduced in 1858. The Probate Registry has been responsible for proving wills and issuing letters of administration from 1858 also, from which date they have been easier to locate from bound volumes (Principal Registry of the Family Division [Probates] London). Wills mostly apply to the more prosperous, of course, who had money or property to leave. Others, such as wives while their husbands were living (before 1882) did not have control of any property. The more prosperous who died intestate were subject to letters of administration, representing about a third of all estates. The same court handled these and, for family historians, similar information is to be found.

More information

Unfortunately there is not a super wills index like the IGI for baptisms, and the records are spread around the record offices. That may mean a lot of effort, as many ancestors might not fall into a particular source. However, even one good find can boost your research as so much information is typically obtained from a will. Each might include a dozen or so other names, and these include friends and business associates as well as relatives – so it is the stuff of real life stories. The document itself is a very personal record, even if actually drafted by a lawyer, sometimes revealing the likes and dislikes, faith and idiosyncrasies of the testator. Like a diary, but probably of greater historical significance, as well as revealing the character of the person, it can give the family historian new leads to fill out an ancestor's life story and its contemporary context.

When reading a will bear in mind abbreviations and the use of common words such as 'father', 'son', 'sister' or 'cousin' we covered earlier. Also you may be surprised at the absence of real estate being passed on as we normally associate with a will. This related to the tenure of land, the fact that an eldest son's inheritance need not be part of the will, and the fact that a married daughter may have had her settlement at the time of marriage. So don't read too much into a miserly bequest to a near relative.

The more you know about the purpose and context of a document the less you are likely to misunderstand it. Classical novels like the Brontës' are excellent background. Download all the leaflets you can find and do a wider search for articles on the web. There is no manageable source of wills and administrations as is the case with vital records, so you will be dependent on all the help you can get. If you are visiting the PRO to locate wills, read the Introductory Note to the PROB 11 class list for background information and help in doing a search.

Court of Probate

From 1858 wills were proved by the Court of Probate, later part of the Supreme Court. These are held at the Probate Search room in central London. You can get copies by post from the Court Service at York for a charge if you have a date of death. You can see microfiche copies of the indices for 1858 to 1993 at the PRO, FRC and the Guildhall library.

Provincial courts

Before 1858 wills were usually proved by one of many church courts and the records are usually held locally, or at one of two archbishops' provincial courts. These are the Prerogative Court of Canterbury (PCC), whose records are held at the PRO; and the Prerogative Court of York (PCY), whose records are held at the Borthwick Institute of Historical Research in York. The York province covers the then counties of Yorkshire, Durham, Northumberland, Westmorland, Cumberland, Lancashire, Cheshire, Nottinghamshire and the Isle of Man. The Canterbury province covered the rest of England and Wales. Records of lesser courts with probate jurisdictions are held at various local records offices. Check with the PRO to see if wills or indices to wills have been published by a record society. Will indexes are listed in Gibson and Churchill's Guide, and most indexes and finding aids are available at the SoG.

The wills in the PCC are covered by name indices. These have been compiled by the Friends of the PRO, the Society of Genealogists etc., covering different historical date ranges. There is no single index, so to find a will at the PRO you will need to check one of the many indices in different formats for different periods. You can get practical information from the PRO reading rooms and the available leaflets.

Note that the will registers at the PRO follow a traditional referencing system. They are numbered by quire – consisting of eight folios, or 16 pages – rather than single page or folio, so you have to look through the whole quire, from its index reference, using the details in the margin.

The texts of almost all wills proved were copied into large parchment registers now available on microfilm, and the vast majority are in English. Most of the probate clauses appended to these texts are in Latin until 1733, but the clause is fairly standard.

More help

Apart from the variety of indices of wills and administrations at the PRO, many other indices, abstracts and 'finding aids' have been published. These have been prepared on different principles such as certain surnames, particular counties or other geographical areas, and certain professions and occupations. Check out the Society of Genealogists' library (covered in Chapter 5) where many are deposited. There is no summary of all these sources. However, many are listed in the publication by J Gibson and E Churchill, *Probate Jurisdications: Where to look for wills*. Even better, if you are lucky with your dates, abstracts or indices of all wills in four individual years (1620, 1630, 1658 and 1750) are covered by separate publications. You can locate copies of these at either the FRC (first three years) or SoG library (1750), but not at the PRO, Kew.

See also the PRO leaflets:
Wills and Death Duty Records After 1858
Wills before 1858: where to start
Probate Records.

Letters of Administration

The Prerogative Courts would grant letters of administration to a person with a claim on an intestate's estate. Probate courts were required to grant administration of the estate to a deceased's widow or next of kin, or a married women to her husband. As we saw earlier, the PCC records are held at the PRO, and the PCY records at the Borthwick Institute in York. PCC grants of administration were registered in the administration act books (PROB 6 at the PRO).

Seats

These were divided into 'seats' reflecting the clerical organisation of the PCC. 'Seats' were the Surrey seat, Welsh seat, Middlesex seat, and London seat, and the Registrar's seat which included testators dying overseas, living outside the province of Canterbury, and other special categories. The administration act books in PROB 6 do not include the full text of individual letters of administration, but summarised, formulaic information unique to each letter. Most of the act books before 1733 are in Latin but clauses tend to be standard.

Inventories

Executors or administrators had to prove to the court that they had carried out their functions properly. This entailed submitting inventories of the deceased's moveable property and expenditure, such as on children and other dependents, over maybe several years. There are indices for these records which provide rich family history pickings. A probate inventory, sometimes extending to several pages, as well as telling us a lot about the deceased persons' affairs, also reflected the social and economic background of the place and time.

Litigation

The PRO also houses the records of will litigation. If your enquiries lead into inheritance disputes you may have soap opera stories to relate. So-called testamentary disputes are featured graphically in J Cox's *Hatred Pursued Beyond the Grave* (HMSO, 1993).

Useful information on other inheritance records at the PRO can be found in the book: *A List of Wills, Administrations, etc. in the Public Record Office, London, England: 12th–19th century*. You will find a copy in the map room at Kew.

IMMIGRANTS TO BRITAIN

Immigrants to Britain over the centuries fell into two categories: those from Ireland and the colonies deemed to have loyalty to the crown; and aliens, or foreigners.

Aliens

Aliens were from 'foreign' countries and acknowledged a different sovereignty and thus had a completely different legal status and fewer rights. Paradoxically, for family history purposes, alien immigrants are much better documented. Irish immigrants were in fact treated as internal migrants so you will not find records of movements, which may in fact have been seasonal because of available work.

Black immigration dates back a long way and there may have been 20,000 Blacks in London alone by the late 18th century. They are not easy to trace from parish registers before 1858 as surnames may not have been included. Clues in the registers are Black nominal references such as 'Pompey' or 'Scipio' and also adult baptism, which was unusual in the Church of England. The PRO has relatively little on West Indian individual immigrants, but you can check the Inward Passenger Lists covering 1878 to 1960. As there are no indices you will need to get an approximate date or port of arrival and do some hard searching. The lists include name, age, occupation and address in the UK. There are also several bibliographical sources that will help in this and other specialist areas.

Indian and Chinese communities have been represented for just about as long as West Indian immigrants, and again it will pay to get some background from the available bibliography if for no other reason than free, detailed information is not quite so abundant on the internet and from the family history organisations. Do a web (browser) search using the name of the country and the word 'genealogy'.

Alien subsidies and certificates of arrival
Mediaeval alien immigrants had to pay double taxes and lists of 'alien subsidies' are held at the PRO. There are three surveys of aliens living in London in November and

December 1571 respectively, and September 1618, published by the Huguenot Society. Many foreigners came from the continent to escape religious persecution of Jews and protestants.

A system of registration of aliens started in 1793, and records include 'certificates of arrival' issued by Justices of the Peace. The certificates give nationality, profession, date of arrival, last country visited and sometimes more information. An index of certificates from 1826 to 1849 is held at the PRO. Other categories of immigration records include denizenship, naturalisation, refugees, and First and Second World War internees and deportees. For these and other categories see the PRO listings and published bibliography.

There is a PRO leaflet *Immigrants*.

EMIGRANTS AND BRITONS ABROAD

In former times British residents had to apply for a licence before going abroad and registers of these exist for the late 16th and early 17th centuries. There are also lists of soldiers taking the oath of allegiance before going abroad to fight, and registers of passengers to New England and other colonies. Another source for British living abroad are the State Papers, Foreign and Colonial, records of the Colonial and Dominions Office, and the Foreign Office Index.

The PRO does not hold internal administrative records of the colonies but each published its own newspapers, or gazettes, and these provide valuable family history information about settlers in addition to basic records. Government gazettes usually include an index. Records of the British in India are not held at the PRO but are among the India Office records at the British Library – there is an index of about 300,000 entries. Another source for Asian emigration is the British Association for Cemeteries in South Asia. The PRO does have certain lists and registers, including the Indian Army List, so include it in your source list on a visit. The PRO has records of military and civilian internees in enemy countries for both World Wars.

North America

Records of immigration into the USA are held in the National Archives in Washington along with census returns, service and other records. The main genealogy websites are US biased so you should have no trouble finding your way in US research. The same applies to French-Canadian records in the Public Archives of Canada. Don't forget the hundreds of local genealogical societies in the USA and Canada that you can join and use as a resource. You can contact the International Society for British Genealogy and Family History, the National Genealogical Society in the USA, and the Family History Association of Canada.

Published information

A lot of the information on emigrants to North America and the West Indies has been published. For example, registers of passengers to New England, Barbados, Maryland, Virginia and other colonies are in print (search for J C Hotten). A short-lived but comprehensive index (1773 and 1776) of new world emigrants from England, Wales and Scotland is held at the PRO, including name, age, occupation, reason for leaving the country, last place of residence, date of departure and destination. Unless you are armed already with 'lucky dates', in such indexed cases weigh the low chance of a hit against the relative ease of a once-for-all search when visiting Kew. Over 17 million immigrant Americans passed through Ellis Island, New York. Go to www.ellisislandrecords.org – you can do a free name search that gives year of arrival and age of passenger.

The Land and Emigration Commission was set up in 1833 to encourage emigration by providing free passages, and you can find the names of emigrants. Outwards Passenger Lists cover those emigrating beyond Europe and the Mediterranean area. These are arranged by year and port of departure and are not yet indexed as I write.

Involuntary emigration

Ancestors having the euphemistic description 'involuntary emigrants', such as transported convicts, are easier to track down than voluntary emigrants. The Colonial Office Emigration Original Correspondence, 1817–1896 contains letters from settlers or intending settlers to British North America, Australia, the West Indies and other places.

Penal settlement

Settlement in Australia began with the penal colony of New South Wales in 1788. The PRO has extensive documentation on transported convicts, and these include voluntary emigrants as sometimes the convict's family also opted to travel. New South Wales Original Correspondence contains lists of settlers and convicts and some are indexed. Censuses were conducted and the fullest is for 1828. You can contact the Society of Australian Genealogists, and special societies for the descendants of transported convicts and 'first fleeters' (do a word search plus 'genealogy').

A fascinating research subject is that of child emigration. Poor children have been subject to involuntary emigration going back to the early 17th century, and the practice was encouraged by Poor Law acts and charities such as Dr Barnados.

Internet emigration links

The following are some useful links in Cyndi's List for researching emigrants from the UK. Go to 'Topical Index', 'General UK Sites', the 'Colonies & Possessions':

- The British Empire
- The British in Singapore and Malaysia
- The British Library – Oriental and India Office Collections
- Cayman-connections Mailing List
  For anyone with a genealogical or historical interest in the Cayman Islands
- Commonwealth War Graves Commission
  Details of 1.7 million members of UK and Commonwealth Forces who died in the 1st and 2nd World Wars and other wars, and 60,000 civilian casualties of WWII. Gives details of grave site, date of death, age, usually parents'/widow's address
- English East India Company Ships
  Shipping losses in the Mercantile Service 1600–1834 (includes Shipwrecks, Captures & Missing Vessels)
- Falkland Island Genealogy
- Family History in India
  For British, European and Anglo-Indian family history in India, Burma, Pakistan and Bangladesh
  ◇ Church records in Colonial India
  ◇ European Cemeteries in India
- Burials in Sirajganj, Bangladesh
- Register of Burials Cinnamara, Assam
  ◇ History of Lascars
    History about Asian seamen working on British Ships
  ◇ Names of Europeans in Colonial India
    Links to over 20,000 names
  ◇ Occupations in Colonial India
- Jute in India
- Hispanic, Central & South America, and the West Indies

Including Mexico, Latin America and the Caribbean
- *Jamaican Ancestry: How to Find Out More*
  A book by Madeleine E. Mitchell
- Jamaican Family Search
- Passages to India – Genealogy Resources in British India
  Includes description of Overland Route to India with P&O SN Company, transcriptions from old newspapers of birth, marriage & death announcements, and info on SOUNDY & SCHAUMBERG families in India
- Researching British Colonies and Dominions
  Information leaflet from the Public Records Office
- The Sun Never Set on the British Empire
  Annotated listing of all the territories & possessions held by Great Britain over time. Excellent for determining where the British were and at what times.
- *Tracing Your West Indian Ancestors*
  A book by Guy Grannum

There are also some PRO leaflets:

Emigrants

Ships' Passenger Lists

Researching British Colonies and Dominions

Emigrants to North America after 1776.

THE ARMED FORCES

The armed services generated prolific records and these will augment the civil records we have covered, and can add a lot of individual flesh to the skeleton of a simple family tree.

Army

The PRO holds War Office records of British soldiers discharged before 1920. A few records date from around the mid-17th century and there is much more information from the mid-18th century to date. This is a rich area of family history and is an instance of where you can investigate the individual lives of your ancestors in some depth. For example, you can read up on specific campaigns in which they were involved and the history of a regiment. In this case go to the relevant bibliography sooner rather than later to build up background knowledge. The PRO has a wide range of books and periodicals. Outside the PRO, sources include the Imperial War Museum, the National Army Museum, the various regimental museums and archives and the Commonwealth War Graves Commission (cwgc.org – you can do a free name search). War deaths are accessible at the FRC in separate registers to civil deaths.

Muster rolls

Before the Civil War (1642–1649) able-bodied men between the ages of 16 and 60 were liable to do military service as the need arose. Many of these 'muster book' records are held in the PRO, and others are in county record offices and private collections. References to individual soldiers occur in wages and widows' pensions records, regimental indices, oaths of allegiance taken, muster rolls and others. As in other cases we have met, especially where records are widely dispersed, it pays to learn a bit about the nature and purpose of the various records and background to the sort of life a soldier lived in different periods and places, and the hierarchical organisation.

Militia lists

After the Civil War a standing army was formed and a bureaucracy that evolved into the War Office. Much better records are available after 1660. The standing army was supplemented by a part-time, county-based militia in the 18th and 19th centuries and these records can be found either in the PRO or county record offices. Although not complete, surviving militia lists (in effect censuses of all men between 18 and 45 from 1758 to 1831) provide information about the men and their family circumstances. The Militia Attestation papers 1806–1816 were completed on recruitment and thereafter formed a full service record. These include date and place of birth so they can be matched to specific ancestors for whom you have that information. Other important sources are the Militia Records 1759–1925, the Military Correspondence 1782–1840 and the Military Entry books 1758–1855. Together these contain a whole variety of information on individual soldiers.

A very wide range of information on commissioned officers is held at the PRO and in the archives of the regiments. Use the information leaflets and record listings to the full, as well as consulting the bibliography for background.

See the range of PRO leaflets with titles commencing 'British Army' and 'British Armed Services' listed in Appendix 1. See also the leaflets:
Tudor and Stuart: Militia Muster Rolls
Mediaeval and Early Modern Soldiers.

Other sources are:
Friends of War Memorials
Crimean War Research Society.

Navy

Various 17th century papers relating to the Navy can be found in the Calendar of State Papers, Domestic at the PRO. Searching is tricky until about the mid-19th century. A good source guide is Rodger's handbook *Naval Records for*

Genealogists. Another, available at the PRO Research Enquires desk is Pappalardo's *Royal Navy Genealogy.* Decide whether you want to just trace a particular lead, dig deeper into an ancestor's life in the military, or treat it as a specialised field of research. If your family tree reveals a naval tradition the subject offers a lifetime of interest on its own, opening up many historical aspects.

See the range of PRO leaflets with titles starting 'Royal Navy' in Appendix 1. There are also leaflets covering the Royal Marines, Merchant Seamen and Merchant Shipping.

PRISONERS AND CRIMINALS

Formal trial records are a poor source of family history. Apart from the wide range of court processes covering an equally wide range of crimes, there is a dearth of indices. It may therefore be more fruitful to trace convicts, such as those transported, and in later periods, prison inmates. More pragmatically, like inquests, crimes attracted newspaper coverage and often long transcripts were included from the trial as well as the 'newsy' sort of family background that family historians are after. When your searches lead to a trial it is probably worth spending time in the bibliography before wading into complex searching.

Crime and punishment

Prison was not always the prime punishment it is today. Offences usually carried the death penalty, which may have been commuted to transportation or reprieved. Relatively few were actually hanged and many incurred fines and/or corporal punishment. County gaols were thus mainly for prisoners awaiting trial. Other prisons, highly localised, were 'for reform purposes' or 'house of correction'. The records are held both at the PRO and at local record offices and a good introduction is Hawkins's *Criminal Ancestors*. There is no central index either of prisoners or convicts.

Habitual criminals and drunkards

Transportation to Australia stopped around 1660, and from that date convicts were imprisoned and subsequently released into the community. To dispel local anxiety, prisons were required to compile registers of 'habitual criminals'. Along with other information, the records also included portraits (another genealogy coup). Centralised national registers were held and some of these are in the PRO, others surviving locally. Consider finding an habitual criminal in your ancestry a family historian's coup (provided the ancestor is not too recent). There are also records of habitual drunkards for the period 1903–1914 if you suspect hereditary leanings. Without transportation, prisons became overcrowded and expensive to administer, so early release was granted by licence, known as 'tickets of leave'. Some of these are covered by indices at the PRO.

The ultimate price

At one point well over 300 offences carried the death penalty although only a small minority of those sentenced were actually hanged, hence pardons and appeals for mercy form a large part of the searchable records. By their nature, petitions for mercy were accompanied by lots of supporting biographical data and are thus a goldmine of family history material. The PRO also has records of executions, as well as contemporary records regarding how the death penalty was implemented.

See PRO leaflets:
British Prisoners of War, c1760–1919
Tracing a 19th Century Criminal in the PRO
Transportation to America and the West Indies 1615–1776
Transportation to Australia 1787–1868
Sources of Convicts and Prisoners
Old Bailey and the Central Criminal Court: Criminal Trials.

CORONERS' INQUESTS

Since the 12th century coroners have been responsible for investigating sudden, unnatural or strange deaths, and deaths in prisons. Records after 1850 have not survived well, and newspaper accounts (it's newsworthy material) may be a better source of information. However, the PRO has many coroners' rolls for the late 13th century to the early 15th century arranged by county. Most modern coroners' records are held in local record offices rather than at the PRO. Records are usually 'closed' for 75 years. Quite a lot has been published by local record societies so it is as well to check with them, as well as the local reference library and the county record office. Even if records for your county have not been published, a publication for another area will usually have a useful background introduction. Another initial resource is Gibson and Rogers's *Coroners' Records in England and Wales.*

See also the PRO Leaflets:
Coroners' Inquests

Inquisitions Post Mortem, Henry III to Charles I: Landholders and their Heirs.

LITIGATION

Law suits are rich in family history information. Records of the Courts of Chancery, Exchequer, Requests and Star Chamber are partly indexed by the Bernau index at the Society of Genealogists. Check out the PRO or SoG websites for the sorts of disputes covered by each court (will disputes, marriage settlements, common lands, mills etc.) and available indices. The Court of Requests allegedly covered 'poor men's causes' against powerful suitors concerning title to property, jointure and marriage contracts etc. The Court of Star Chamber was concerned with law and order. There are cases for example, about the goods of suicides.

See PRO leaflets:
Court of Star Chamber, 1845–1642
Court of Requests, 1845–1642: A Court for the "Poor"
Chancery Proceedings: Equity Suits from 1558
Chancery: Masters' Reports and certificates.

THE ESTABLISHED CHURCH

The PRO holds records concerning church clergy and laity before and after the Reformation. Although not in vast numbers, examples of records of interest to family historians are excommunicates and sacrament certificates. From 1672 various enactments required certain office holders and aliens seeking naturalisation to take oaths in support of the crown and against papal supremacy. This entailed taking the sacrament according to Anglican rites and a sacrament certificate was issued.

Excommunication from the church covered a wide variety of offences and 'requests' ('significations' or *significavits*) included this information, *inter alia*, about the individual. Research involving the clergy can start with Crockford's Clerical Directory, published annually since 1858. Ordination records in the local diocesan archives are especially informative and include, probably, a copy of baptism entry, education and character reference.

Resource links on Cyndi's List:
Religions and Churches
Brief History of the Church of England
UK Church Directory.

See also PRO leaflet: *Oath Rolls and Sacrament Certificates after 1660.*

NONCONFORMISTS

The PRO holds most nonconformist registers of births, deaths and marriages before civil registration was introduced in 1837 and many after that date. Consult the specialist guide published by the PRO: *Protestant Nonconformity and Roman Catholicism* (Shorney). Huguenots, French Protestants fleeing from religious persecution, settled in Britain from the 1550s onwards, in certain localities (excluding the midlands, north of England and Scotland). The Huguenot library will undertake a brief search for a fee.

The SoG have a range of publications on nonconformist family history:

- My Ancestors Were Baptists: How Can I Find Out More About Them?
- My Ancestors Were Congregationalists in England and Wales: How Can I Find Out More About Them?
- My Ancestors Were English Presbyterians/Unitarians: How Can I Find Out More About Them?
- My Ancestors Were Methodists: How Can I Find Out More About Them?
- My Ancestors Were in the Salvation Army: How Can I Find Out More About Them?
- My Ancestors Were Quakers: How Can I Find Out More About Them?
- The Salvations Army – How can I trace information about my Salvationist ancestors

Other resource links via Cyndi's List:

Britain Yearly Meetings (Quakers)
Baptist Historical Society
Baptist Union of Great Britain
ExLIBRIS: English Dissenters
Find a Church – The UK Church Directory
Methodist Church of Great Britain (Official Website)
United Reformed Church.

ROMAN CATHOLICS

The registers of Catholic churches are either with the PRO or the churches. The Catholic Central Library or the relevant diocesan archivist should be able to help with research. Also the Catholic Record Society has published lots of useful material in respect of the UK and Ireland, and the publication *English Catholic Ancestor* acquires and disseminates information about Catholic families. Try also the Catholic Family History Society, Catholic Archives Society (UK and

Ireland). Catholics were allowed to worship in their own churches from 1791 but had to marry in Anglican churches (only Anglican marriages were legal after the introduction of Hardwickes's Marriage Act of 1754). Catholic burials may have taken place in the parish churchyard so will be in the parish registers. For more background search the bibliography on Catholic family history *at amazon.co.uk*

JEWS

The London and Metropolitan Archives has a wide collection of archives on Jewish settlement in London and the UK, and the Society of Genealogists also has records. The names and addresses of synagogues throughout the British Isles are in the *Jewish Year Book* and you can get help generally from the Board of Deputies, Jewish Information Department. The United Synagogue has records from the main London synagogues founded before 1837 and you can search these for a fee. The Anglo-Jewish Association and the Jewish Genealogical Society of Great Britain may also be able to help.

No records date back before the expulsion of Jews in 1290, but you can get information abut that early community in the PRO Guide. Two sorts of immigrants can be researched: Sephardim were Portuguese, Italian and Spanish arriving from 1656 onwards; Ashkenazim were from Central and Eastern Europe, arriving from the 1680s. A large wave of Ashkenazim were Russians and Poles arriving towards the end of the nineteenth century. The PRO Guide and above resources should be enough to get you off to a confident start in this specialised area.

THE POOR

From the time of the Elizabeth Poor Laws of 1601 paupers were a charge on the local parish 'of settlement' (birth or husband's birth) and local taxes were raised for their support. There is not much at the PRO covering Poor Law records. The local county record office will have these, and they provide important family history information. The Poor Law Amendment Act of 1834 set up workhouses that supplied indoor relief with a view to making such a course a very last resort, thus keeping down local taxes for the purpose. Several parishes were grouped into unions, which are the areas of administration you will meet in your research. Get hold of the pamphlets by Gibson and Young as an introduction and guide to the local records.

See also the PRO leaflets:
Poor Law Records 1834–1871
Poor Laws and the Poor.

LAND OWNERSHIP

Before the 19th century, records of land transactions are hard to locate. However, thousands of records are held by the PRO, mainly in respect of land at some time in the possession of the crown, land affected by litigation, and where a transfer was enrolled in a court's records as proof of ownership. As with other major sources of public records, the absence of centralised record systems, and/or the absence of current indices, means that the researcher has to gather information about the nature and purpose of the records to have a fighting chance of finding specific family history information. Background information is usually available in the bibliography and from articles and guides.

Surveys of property – mainly comprising so-called 'rentals' and 'surveys' – date from the 13th century but most that exist are from the 16th and 17th centuries. These were mainly for the purpose of manorial estate management, as a record of tenants and revenue value. The PRO holds published lists of surveys under Lists of Rentals and Surveys (plus an addendum). Manorial accounts recorded rental transactions and these are termed ministers' and receivers' accounts. Various Lists of Ministers' Accounts can be seen at the PRO. More of these have survived than surveys, as they were compiled annually.

See the range of PRO leaflets with titles starting *Land Conveyances* in Appendix 1.

TAX

After the age of 14, unless he or she begged for a living, your ancestor might have been liable for one or more taxes and this area can be informative about individuals. Many old taxation records have been published by local societies, so in this case it is worth checking from the PRO what is in print before trying to locate individual sources and documents. Mullins's Texts and Calandars is a list of such publications. You can get information on hearth taxes, lay subsidies, poll taxes and others from the PRO.

See the PRO leaflets:
Taxation Records Before 1660
Tithe Records. A Detailed Examination.

NAME CHANGES

Anyone can legally change their name without bringing attention to the fact unless it is for the intention of defrauding. Where the change is recorded it may be by deed poll, a statutory declaration or a newspaper advertisement. So depending on whether and how a name change was recorded this can present researchers with tricky challenges. This is a minor source of public records but may be very significant to genealogists. We discussed name changes in Chapter 7.

WELSH GENEALOGY

Welsh research faces a few extra problems. Inherited surnames came later than in England, and a relatively small number of names (including Jones, Evans, Davies and Thomas) emerged. Most of the Welsh record offices produce their own genealogical leaflets as does the Welsh Tourist Office. The National Library holds many parish registers and transcripts as well as wills, deeds, personal and estate records and the records of Welsh courts before 1830. *The Golden Grove Book of Pedigrees* is an early eighteenth century genealogical collection now in the care of the Carmarthenshire Archives Service. Most of the records sources already described will be as helpful in locating Welsh ancestors as English. Consider checking hearth records of the late 17th century. For Welsh births, deaths and marriages go to the FRC.

Because of the strong noncomformist tradition in Wales this category of records may prove especially productive. They are arranged by county then denomination. Census records are also arranged by place and there are lots of Welsh history records at Kew. The University of Wales, Board of Celtic

Studies has published a *History and Law* series covering legal disputes and these are well indexed. Also check out the *Bernau Index* at the Society of Genealogists, and the assize records in the National Library. You can locate Welsh army records from the territorial basis of regiments. For earlier Welsh records look at the PRO Guide.

This and the following national record categories are covered very briefly as you can get plenty of information from high level links in all the main genealogy websites, such as GENUKI and Cyndi's List. At national level there is also a plentiful bibliography. In any case, so much of what you will learn about family history and searching methods applies across the board so does not require repetition.

SCOTTISH GENEALOGY

Civil registration of births, deaths and marriages began in 1855 – later than in England. The records, along with many parish registers, are held by the Registrar General in Edinburgh and can be searched for a fee. The indices can also be searched by computer at the FRC (Scottish Link) for an hourly fee, or also for a charge on the web. This gives access to all births, marriages and deaths records since 1855, plus adoptions and divorces and indices to censuses for 1881 and 1891. Also computerised are the Scottish Church registers of births, baptisms and marriages from 1555 to 1854. The Society of Genealogists has an extensive range of Scottish records. As with Welsh archives, army searches are made easy because of the territorial basis of regiments. Go to the PRO website for details of the many Scottish records they hold, and check out scotsorigin.net.

IRISH GENEALOGY

Many Irish records were lost in a fire at the Irish Public Record Office in 1922 and, sooner or later, this will affect most researchers into Irish genealogy. Of population censuses taken every ten years between 1821 and 1911, those from 1861 to 1891 were destroyed by the government and most of the others were lost in the fire. The general rule is to make a preliminary approach to the Irish Genealogical Research Society for help, and perhaps to consult some of the bibliography on the subject (*amazon.co.uk*) before you start. Unlike English censuses, the early Irish ones included names, so it's swings and roundabouts. A census for the Republic was taken in 1926 and this is open to public inspection. Returns for 1901 and 1911 are also complete and open for inspection.

Civil registration of marriages other than Roman Catholic started in 1845 and the civil registration of births, deaths and all marriages started in 1864. Records for the whole of Ireland up to 1921, and the Republic since that date, are held in the General Register Office of Ireland in Dublin. The records for Northern Ireland are held in the General Register Office of Northern Ireland in Belfast. There are separate register offices for births, deaths and marriages occurring outside Ireland, the equivalent of the 'English and Welsh abroad' PRO records.

Irish parish registers are also very incomplete, and the IGI includes about 2 million names. Many of the Anglican Church of Ireland parish registers were lost in the 1922 fire, and were in any case used only by a minority of the population. Roman Catholic parish registers mostly date back no further than 1830. You can check with the Society of

Genealogists for the registers they have and GENUKI for locating Irish records generally. Nearly all probate records before 1904 were destroyed in 1922, although surviving 'vicar's indices' give a clue as to what they contained. Calendars of wills proved and administrations granted since 1858 can be seen at the National Archives and PRONI, which has extracts of many Ulster wills. The Ulster Historical Foundation will conduct searches.

Some archive 'calendars' had been published before the fire of 1922 and these can be seen in the PRO library at Kew. Also, a wealth of historical data is covered in the State Papers, Ireland, and at the General Register Office in Belfast. This data is well indexed and in précis form – you can check out their catalogue for details. Fortunately a lot of Irish genealogy can be done from the PRO and other records outside Ireland. As well as the PRO, GENUKI and Cindi's List websites have prolific Irish genealogy links.

Appendix 1

INSTANT INFORMATION
Public Record Office
Leaflets and Document Archives

Admiralty Charts (Maps)

Agricultural Statistics, from 1866 onwards: Parish Summaries

American and West Indian Colonies before 1782

American Revolution

Anglo-Jewish History: Sources in the PRO, 18th–20th Centuries

Apprenticeship Records as Sources for Genealogy

Architectural Drawings in the PRO

Assizes (English), 1656–1971: Key to Series for Civil Trials

Assizes (English), Key for Criminal Trials, 1559–1971

Assizes: Criminal Trials

Auxiliary Army Forces: Volunteers, Yeomanry, Territorials & Home Guard 1769–1945

Bankruptcy Records after 1869

Bankrupts and Insolvent Debtors:1710–1869

Births, Marriages and Deaths at Sea

British Armed Services: Campaign Medals, and other Service Medals

British Armed Services: Gallantry Medals

British Armed Services: Gallantry Medals, Further Information

British Army List

British Army Officers' Records: First World War 1914–1918

British Army Soldiers' Papers: First World War 1914–1918

British Army War Diaries: First World War, 1914–1918

British Army: Campaign Records, 1660–1714

British Army: Campaign Records, 1714–1815

British Army: Courts Martial, 17th–20th Centuries

British Army: Courts Martial; First World War, 1914–1918

British Army: Muster Rolls and Pay Lists, c1730–1898

British Army: Nurses and Nursing Services

British Army: Officers' Records 1660–1913

British Army: Officers' Commissions

British Army: Operational Records 1816–1913

British Army: Operations after 1945

British Army: Soldiers' Discharge Papers, 1760–1913

British Army: Soldiers' Pensions, 1702–1913

British Army: Useful Sources for Tracing Soldiers

British Prisoners of War, c1760–1919

Royal Grants: Letters Patent and Charters, 1199–Present Day

Royal Household and Wardrobe Before 1660

Royal Irish Constabulary Records

Royal Marines: Further Areas of Research

Royal Marines: How to Find a Division

Royal Marines: Officers' Service Records

Royal Marines: Other Ranks' Service Records

Royal Naval Dockyards

Royal Naval Research and Development

Royal Naval Reserve

Royal Naval Volunteer Reserve

Royal Navy: Log Books and Reports of Proceedings

Royal Navy: Nurses and Nursing Services

Royal Navy: Officers' Service Records

Royal Navy: Officers' Service Records, First World War, and Confidential Reports, 1893–1942

Royal Navy: Operational Records

Royal Navy: Operational Records 1660–1914

Royal Navy: Operational Records, First World War, 1914–1918

Royal Navy: Pay and Pension Records: Commissioned Officers

Royal Navy: Pension Records: Ratings

Royal Navy: Pension Records: Warrant Officers

Royal Navy: Ratings Entering Service Between 1873 and 1923

Royal Navy: Ratings' Service Records 1667–1923

Royal Warrant Holders and Household Servants

Royal Warrant Holders, and Suppliers of Goods, from 1660

Seals

Second World War, 1939–1945: the War Cabinet

Second World War: British Army Operations 1939–1945

Ships Wrecked or Sunk

Ships' Passenger Lists, 1878–1960

Sources for the History of Mines and Quarries

Sources for the History of Religious Houses and Their Lands, c.1000–1530

Sources of Convicts and Prisoners 1100–1986

State Papers, Domestic: The Commonwealth, 1642–1660

State Papers, Domestic: Charles II–Anne 1660–1714

State Papers, Domestic: Edward VI–Charles 1, 1547–1649

State Papers, Domestic: George I to George III, 1714–1782

State Papers, Domestic: Miscellaneous Classes

State Papers, Ireland, 1509–1782

State Papers, Foreign

Stationers' Hall Copyright Records

Supreme Court, Chancery Division: Cases after 1875

Supreme Court: Appeal Cases After 1875

Taxation Records before 1660

Titanic

Tithe Records: A Detailed Examination

Appendix 2

HELP AND SUPPORT
Local Family History Societies

BEDFORDSHIRE
Bedfordshire FHS
    CONTACT: Mrs Pauline Redpath, PO Box 214, Bedford MK42 9RX
    E-MAILS: bfhs@bfhs. org. uk
    WEB-SITE: www.bfhs.org.uk <http://www.bfhs.org.uk/>

BERKSHIRE
Berkshire FHS
    CONTACT: Mr J Gurnett, 5 Wren Close, Burghfield Common,
    Berkshire, RG7 3PF
    E-MAILS: secretary@berksfhs. org.uk
    WEB-SITE: www.berksfhs.org.uk <http://www.berksfhs.org.uk/>

BUCKINGHAMSHIRE
Buckinghamshire FHS
    CONTACT: c/o PO Box 403, Aylesbury, Buckinghamshire HP21 7GU
    WEB-SITE: www bucksfhs.org.uk <http://www.bucksfhs.org.uk/>

CAMBRIDGESHIRE
Cambridgeshire FHS
    CONTACT: Mrs Ann Thompson, 2 Offa Lea, Newton, CAMBRIDGE
    CB2 5PW (changed NOV2001)
    E-MAILS: michaelandann@offalea.fsnet.co.uk (added NOV2001)
    WEB-SITE: www.cfhs.org.uk <http:www.cfhs.org.uk/>

Cambridge University H&GS
    CONTACT: c/o Crossfield House, Dale Road, Stanton, Bury St
    Edmunds, Suffolk IP31 2DY
    E-MAILS: njb25@hermes.cam.ac.uk
    WEB-SITE: www.cam.ac.uk/societies/cuhags
    <http://www.cam.ac.uk/societies/cuhags/>

CHANNEL ISLANDS
Channel Islands FHS
   CONTACT: Mrs S Payn, PO Box 507, St Helier, Jersey JE4 5TN
   WEB-SITE: user.itl.net/~glen/AbouttheChannelIslandsFHS.html
   <http://user.itl.net/~glen/AbouttheChannelIslandsFHS.html>

La Soc Guernesiaise (FH Section)
   CONTACT: The Secretary, PO Box 314, Candie, St Peter Port,
   Guernsey, GY1 3TG
   WEB-SITE: www.societe.org.gg/sections/family/historysec.htm
   <http://www.societe.org.gg/sections/familyhistorysec.htm>

CHESHIRE
The FHS of Cheshire
   CONTACT: Mrs H Massey, 101 Irby Road, Heswall, Wirral,
   Merseyside L61 6UZ
   E-MAILS: info@fhsc.org.uk
   WEB-SITE: www.fhsc.org.uk <http://www.fhsc.org.uk/>

North Cheshire FHS
   CONTACT: Mrs Rhoda Clarke, 2 Denham Drive, Bramhall, Stockport,
   Cheshire SK7 2AT
   WEB-SITE: www.genuki.org.uk/big/eng/CHS/NorthChesFHS
   <http://www.genuki.org.uk/big/eng/CHS/NorthChesFHS/>

South Cheshire FHS
   CONTACT: PO Box 1990, Crew, Cheshire CW2 6FF
   WEB-SITE: www.scfhs.org.uk <http://www.scfhs.org.uk/>

CORNWALL
Cornwall FHS
   CONTACT: The Administrator, 5 Victoria Square, Truro, Cornwall
   TR1 2RS
   E-MAILS: secretary@cornwallfhs.com
   WEB-SITE: www.cornwallfhs.com <http://www.cornwallfhs.com>

CUMBERLAND
Cumbria FHS
   CONTACT: Mrs M Russell, 32 Granada Road, Denton, Manchester
   M34 2IJ
   WEB-SITE: www.genuki.org.uk/big/eng/CUL/cumbFHS
   <http://www.genuki.org.uk/big/eng/CUL/cumbFHS/>
   Also listed under WESTMORLAND

Furness FHS
   CONTACT: Miss J Fairbairn, 64 Cowlarns Road, Barrow-in-Furness,
   Cumbria LA14 4HJ
   E-MAILS: julia.fairbairn@virgin.net
   WEB-SITE: members.aol.com/FurnessFHS/fpw.htm
   <http://members.aol.com/FurnessFHS/fpw.htm>
   Also listed under LANCASHIRE

DERBYSHIRE
Derbyshire FHS
   CONTACT: Mr G Wells, Bridge Chapel House, St Mary's Bridge,
   Sowter Rd, Derby DE1 3AT
   WEB-SITE: www.dfhs.org.uk <http://www.dfhs.org.uk/>

Chesterfield & District HFS
   CONTACT: Mrs Dorothy Flaxman, 16 Mill Crescent, Wingerworth,
   Chesterfield, Derbyshire S42 6NN (changed APR2002)
   E-MAILS: cadfhs@aol.com (changed APR2002)

DEVON
Devon FHS
   CONTACT: The Secretary, Devon FHS, PO Box 9, Exeter, Devon
   EX2 6YP
   E-MAILS: secretary@devonfhs.org.uk
   WEB-SITE: www.devonfhs.org.uk <http://www.devonfhs.org.uk/>

DORSET
Dorset FHS
   CONTACT: Mrs Debbie Winter, 131 Lynwood Drive, Merley,
   Wimborne, Dorset, BH21 1UU
   E-MAILS: contact@Dorsetfhs.freeserve.co.uk (added NOV2001)
   WEB-SITE: www.dorsetfhs.freeserve.co.uk
   <http://www. dorsetfhs.freeserve.co.uk> (changed NOV2001)

Somerset & Dorset FHS
   CONTACT: The Secretary, PO Box 4502 Sherborne DT9 6YL
   E-MAILS: society@sdfhs.org
   WEB-SITE: www.sdfhs.org <http://www.sdfhs.org>
   Also listed under SOMERSET

DURHAM

Cleveland, N.Yorkshire & S. Durham FHS
  CONTACT: Mr A Sampson, 1 Oxgang Close, Redcar, Cleveland TS10
  4ND
  WEB-SITE: website.lineone.net/~pjoiner/cfhs/cfhs.html
  <http://website.lineone.net/~pjoiner/cfhs/cfhs.html>
  Also listed under YORKSHIRE – North Riding

Northumberland & Durham FHS
  CONTACT: Mrs Frances Norman, 23 Monkton Avenue, Simonside,
  South Shields, Tyne & Wear, NE34 9RX
  E-MAILS: frances@fnorman.fsnet.co.uk
  WEB-SITE: www.ndfhs.org.uk <http://www.ndfhs.org.uk/> (changed
  MCH2002)
  Also listed under NORTHUMBERLAND

ESSEX

Essex SFH
  CONTACT: Mrs A Church, Windyridge, 32 Parsons Heath, Colchester,
  Essex CO4 3HX
  E-MAILS: secretary@esfh.org.uk (added NOV2001)
  WEB-SITE: www.esfh.org.uk <http://www.esfh.org.uk/>

East of London FHS
  CONTACT: Mrs Judith Taylor, 42 Alwen Grove, Sth Ockendon, Essex
  RM15 5DW
  WEB-SITE: eolfhs.rootsweb.com <http://eolfhs.rootsweb.com>
  Also listed under LONDON (Greater London)

Waltham Forest FHS
  CONTACT: Mr B F Burton, 49 Sky Peals Rd, Woodford Green, Essex
  IG8 9NE
  Also listed under LONDON (Greater London)

GLOUCESTERSHIRE

Gloucestershire FHS
  CONTACT: Mrs Sue Stafford, 4 Twyver Close, Upton St Leonards,
  Gloucestershire GL4 8EF
  E-MAILS: glosearch@hotmail.com
  WEB-SITE: www.cix.co.uk/~rd/GENUKI/gfhs.htm
  <http://www.cix.co.uk/~rd/GENUKI/gfhs.htm>

Bristol & Avon FHS
 CONTACT: Mrs Audrey Lovell, 784 Muller Road, Eastville, Bristol,
 BS5 6XA
 WEB-SITE: www.bafhs.org.uk <http://www.bafhs.org.uk>
 lAlso listed under SOMERSET

HAMPSHIRE
Hampshire Genealogical Society
 CONTACT: Mrs Sue Smith, Oakbourne, Uplands Road, Denmead,
 Hants PO7 6HE
 E-MAILS: secretary@hgs-online.org.uk
 WEB-SITE: www.hgs-online.org.uk <http://www.hgs-online.org.uk/>

Isle of Wight FHS
 CONTACT: Mrs Betty Dhillon, Spindrift, 3 Milne Way, Newport,
 IOW PO30 1YF
 E-MAILS: betty.dhillon@btinternet.com
 WEB-SITE: www.dina.clara.net/iosfhs
 <http://www.dina.clara.net/iowfhs/>
 Also listed under ISLE OF WIGHT

HEREFORDSHIRE
Herefordshire FHS
 CONTACT: Mr Brian Prosser, 6 Birch Meadow, Gosmore Road,
 Clehonger, Hereford HR2 9RH
 E-MAILS: prosser_brian@hotmail.com
 WEB-SITE: www.rootsweb.com/~ukhfhs
 <http://www.rootsweb.com/~ukhfhs/>

HERTFORDSHIRE
Hertfordshire Family & Population HS
 CONTACT: Mr Ken Garner, 2 Mayfair Close, St Albans, Herts
 AL4 9TN
 E-MAILS: secretary@hertsfhs.org.uk (changed DEC2001)
 WEB-SITE: www.hertsfhs.org.uk <http://www.hertsfhs.org.uk/>
 (changed DEC2001)

Royston & District FHS
   CONTACT: Mrs Joyce Hellier, 60 Heathfield, Royston, Hertfordshire
   SG8 5BN
   WEB-SITE:
   www.hertsdirect.org/infoadvice/leisure/activities/hthist3y/776446
   <http://www.hertsdirect.org/infoadvice/leisure/activities/hthist3y/776446>

Letchworth & District FH Group
   CONTACT: Mrs D M Paterson, 84 Kings Hedges, Hitchin, Herts
   SG5 2QE
   WEB-SITE:
   www.hertsdirect.org/infoadvice/leisure/activities/hthist3y/748109
   <http:/www.hertsdirect.org/inforadvice/leisure/activities/hthist3y/748109>

HUNTINGDONSHIRE
Huntingdon FHS
   CONTACT: Mrs C Kesseler, 42 Crowhill, Godmanchester,
   Huntingdon, Cambs PE29 2NR
   E-MAILS: secretary@huntsfhs.org.uk (changed DEC2001)
   WEB-SITE: www.huntsfhs.org.uk <http://www.huntsfhs.org.uk/>
   (changed DEC2001)

ISLE OF MAN
Isle of Man FHS
   CONTACT: Mr E W Q Cleator, 5 Selborne Drive, Douglas, Isle of
   Man
   WEB-SITE: www.isle-of-man.com/interests/genealogy/fhs
   <http://www.isle-of-man.com/interests/genealogy/fhs/>

ISLE of WIGHT
Isle of Wight FHS
   CONTACT: Mrs Betty Dhillon, Spindrift, 3 Milne Way, Newport,
   IOW PO30 1YF
   E-MAILS: betty.dhillon@btinternet.com
   WEB-SITE: www.dina.clara.net/iowfhs
   <http://www.dina.clara.net/iowfhs/>
   Also listed under HAMPSHIRE

KENT
Folkestone & District FHS
  CONTACT: Mrs Levina B Jones, Brickwall Farmhouse, Bengemarsh
  Road, Lydd, Kent TN29 9JH
  E-MAILS: levina.jones@virgin.net
  WEB-SITE:
  freespace.virgin.net/jennifer.killick/Folkestone&DistrictFHS
  <http://freespace.virgin.net/jennifer.killick/Folkestone&DistrictFHS/>

Kent FHS
  CONTACT: Mrs Kristin Slater, Bullockstone Farm, Bullockstone
  Road, Herne, Kent CT6 7NL
  E-MAILS: kristn@globalnet.co.uk
  WEB-SITE: www.kfhs.org.uk <http://www.kfhs.org.uk/>

North West Kent FHS
  CONTACT: Mrs S Rhuss, 6 Windermere Road, Barnhurst,
  Bexleyheath, Kent DA7 6PW
  E-MAILS: secretary@nwkfhs.org.uk
  WEB-SITE: www.nwkfhs.org.uk <http://www.nwkfhs.org.uk/>
  Also listed under LONDON (Greater London)

Tunbridge Wells FHS
  CONTACT: Mrs Oxenbury, The Old Cottage, Langton Road,
  Tunbridge Wells, Kent TN3 0BA
  E-MAILS: brian@kcckal.demon.co.uk
  WEB-SITE: www.kcckal.demon.co.uk/twfhsmain.htm
  <http://www.kcckal.demon.co.uk/twfhsmain.htm>

Woolwich & District FHS
  CONTACT: Mrs Edna Reynolds, 54 Parkhill Road, Bexley, Kent
  DA5 1HY
  E-MAILS: FrEdnaFHS@cs.com (added JAN2002)
  Also listed under LONDON (Greater London)

LANCASHIRE
Furness FHS
  CONTACT: Miss J Fairbairn, 64 Cowlarns Road, Barrow-in-Furness,
  Cumbria LA14 4HJ
  E-MAILS: julia.fairbairn@virgin.net
  WEB-SITE: members.aol.com/FurnessFHS/fpw.htm
  <http://members.aol.com/FurnessFHS/fpw.htm>
  Also listed under CUMBERLAND

Lancashire FH & HS
CONTACT: Mrs J Huntingdon, 15 Christ Church Street, Accrington,
Lancs BB5 2LZ
E-MAILS: jehuntingdon@08002go.com
WEB-SITE: www.lancashire-fhhs.org.uk
<http://www.lancashire-fhhs.org.uk/>

Lancashire Parish Register Society
CONTACT: Mr Tom O'Brien, 135 Sandy Lane, Orford, Warrington
WA2 9JB (address changed DEC2001)
E-MAILS: Tom_OBrien@bigfoot.com
WEB-SITE: www.genuki.org.uk/big/eng/LAN/lprs
<http://www.genuki.org.uk/big/eng/LAN/lprs/>

Lancashire FH Group
CONTACT: Mrs M. Wilmshurst, 94 Croston Road, Garstang, Preston,
Lancs PR3 1HR

Liverpool & SW Lancs FHS
CONTACT: Mr David Guiver, 11 Bushbys Lane, Formby, Liverpool
L37 2DX
WEB-SITE: www.liverpool-genealogy.org.uk
<http://www.liverpool-genealogy.org.uk/> (changed JAN2002)

Manchester & Lancs FHS
CONTACT: Mr John Marsden, c/o M&LFHS, Clayton House, 59
Piccadilly, Manchester M1 2AQ (changed DEC2001)
WEB-SITE: www.mlfhs.demon.co.uk
<http://www.mlfhs.demon.co.uk/>

North Meols FHS
CONTACT: Mrs Nadine Taylor, 9 The Paddock, Ainsdale, Southport,
Lancs PR8 3PT
WEB-SITE: www.users.zetnet.co.uk/nmfhs
<http://www.users.zetnet.co.uk/nmfhs>

Ormskirk & District FHS
CONTACT: Avril Freeman, c/o Ormskirk College, Hants Lane,
Ormskirk, Lancs L39 1PX

Wigan F&LHS
    CONTACT: Brian Fairhurst, 615 Wigan Road, Bryn, Wigan, Lancs
    WN4 0BY
    E-MAILS: Brifair6l@aol.com (added MCH2002)
    WEB-SITE: www.ffhs.org.uk/members/wigan.htm
    <http://www.ffhs.org.uk/members/wigan.htm> (added MCH2002)

LEICESTERSHIRE
Leicestershire & Rutland FHS
    CONTACT: Ray Broad, 11 Spring Lane, Wymondham, Leicestershire
    LE14 2AY
    E-MAILS: ray.broad@ntlworld.com
    WEB-SITE: feepages.genealogy.rootsweb.com/~leicsrut
    <http://freepages.genealogy.rootsweb.com/~leicsrut/>
    Also listed under RUTLAND

LINCOLNSHIRE
Isle of Axholme FHS
    CONTACT: A B Wise, Alwinton, 51 Mill Road, Crowle, Isle of
    Axholme, North Lincolnshire DN17 4LW
    E-MAILS: Alwinton51@btinternet.com
    WEB-SITE: www.linktop.demon.co.uk/axholme
    <http://www.linktop.demon.co.uk/axholme/>

Lincolnshire FHS
    CONTACT: Colin E Baslington, 1 Pennygate Gardens, Spalding,
    Lincolnshire PE11 1XJ
    E-MAILS: LINfhsSec@aol.com
    WEB-SITE: www.genuki.org.uk/big/eng/LIN/lfhs
    <http://www.genuki.org.uk/big/eng/LIN/lfhs/>

LONDON (GREATER LONDON)
East of London FHS
    CONTACT: Mrs Judith Taylor, 42 Alwen Grove, Sth Ockendon, Essex
    RM15 5DW
    WEB-SITE: eolfhs.rootsweb.com <http://eolfhs.rootsweb.com>
    Also listed under ESSEX

East Surrey FHS
    CONTACT: Mrs Marion Brackpool, 370 Chipstead Valley Road,
    Coulsdon, Surrey CR5 3BF
    WEB-SITE: www.eastsurreyfhs.org.uk
    <http://www.eastsurreyfhs.org.uk>
    Also listed under SURREY

Hillingdon FHS
    CONTACT: Mrs G May, 20 Moreland Drive, Gerrards Cross, Bucks
    SL9 8BB
    E-MAILS: Gillmay@dial.pipex.com
    WEB-SITE: users.rootsweb.com/~enghfhs
    <http://users.rootsweb.com/~enghfhs/>
    Also listed under MIDDLESEX

London & North Middlesex FHS
    incorporating the Westminster & Central Middlesex FHS
    CONTACT: Mrs S. Lumas, 7 Mount Pleasant Road, New Malden,
    Surrey KT3 3JZ
    WEB-SITE: www.lnmfhs.dircon.co.uk
    <http://www.lnmfhs.dircon.co.uk/>
    Also listed under MIDDLESEX

North West Kent FHS
    CONTACT: Mrs S Rhys, 6 Windermere Road, Barnhurst, Bexleyheath,
    Kent DA7 6PW
    E-MAILS: secretary@nwkfhs.org.uk
    WEB-SITE: www.nwkfhs.org.uk <http://www.nwkfhs.org.uk/>
    Also listed under KENT

Waltham Forest FHS
    CONTACT: Mr B F Burton, 49 Sky Peals Road, Woodford Green,
    Essex IG8 9NE
    Also listed under ESSEX

West Middlesex FHS
    CONTACT: Mrs Mavis Burton, 10 West Way, Heston, Middlesex,
    TW5 0JF
    WEB-SITE: www.west-middlesex-fhs.org.uk
    <http://www.west-middlesex-fhs.org.uk>
    Also listed under MIDDLESEX

Westminster & Central Middlesex FHS
Please see under LONDON & NORTH MIDDLESEX FHS

Woolwich & District FHS
CONTACT: Mrs Edna Reynolds, 54 Parkhill Road, Bexley, Kent
DA5 1HY
E-MAILS: FrEdnaFHS@cs.com (added JAN2002)
Also listed under KENT

MIDDLESEX
Hillingdon FHS
CONTACT: Mrs G May, 20 Moreland Drive, Gerrards Cross, Bucks
SL9 8BB
E-MAILS: Gillmay@dial.pipex.com
WEB-SITE: users.rootsweb.com/~enghfhs
<http://users.rootsweb.com~/enghfhs/>
Also listed under LONDON (Greater London)

London & North Middlesex FHS
incorporating the Westminster & Central Middlesex FHS
CONTACT: Mrs S Lumas, 7 Mount Pleasant Road, New Malden,
Surrey KT3 3JZ
WEB-SITE: www.lnmfhs.dircon.co.uk <http://lnmfhs.dircon.co.uk/>
Also listed under LONDON (Greater London)

West Middlesex FHS
CONTACT: Mrs Mavis Burton, 10 West Way, Heston, Middlesex
TW5 0JF
WEB-SITE: www.west-middlesex-fhs.org.uk
<http://www.west-middlesex-fhs.org.uk>
Also listed under LONDON (Greater London)

Westminster & Central Middlesex FHS
Please see under LONDON & NORTH MIDDLESEX FHS

NORFOLK
Norfolk FHS
CONTACT: Mrs Rhona Kerswell, Kirby Hall, 70 St Giles Street,
Norwich, NR2 1LS
E-MAILS: nfhs@paston.co.uk
WEB-SITE: www.norfolkfhs.org.uk/ <http://www.norfolkfhs.org.uk/>
(address changed DEC2001)

Mid-Norfolk FHS
  CONTACT: Mrs Melanie Donnelly, Codgers Cottage, 6 Hale Road,
  Bradenham, Thetford, Norfolk IP25 7RA
  E-MAILS: melaniedonnelly@codgerscottage.fsnet.co.uk
  WEB-SITE:
  www.uea.ac.uk/~s300/genuki/NFK/organisations/midnfhs/>
  http://www.uea.ac.uk~s300/genuki/NFK/organisations/midnfhs/7

NORTHAMPTONSHIRE
Northamptonshire FHS
  CONTACT: Mrs Jean Rolfe, 2 Yew Tree Court, Boothville,
  Northampton NN3 6SF (changed JAN2002)
  WEB-SITE: www.fugazi.demon.co.uk/index.htm
  <http://www.fugazi.demon.co.uk/index.htm> (changed JAN2002)

Peterborough & District FHS
  CONTACT: Mrs Pauline Kennelly, 33 Farleigh Fields, Orton Wistow,
  Peterborough PE2 6YB

NORTHUMBERLAND
Northumberland & Durham FHS
  CONTACT: Mrs Frances Norman, 23 Monkton Avenue, Simonside,
  South Shields, Tyne & Wear, NE34 9RX
  E-MAILS: frances@fnorman.fsnet.co.uk
  WEB-SITE: www.ndfhs.org.uk <http://www.ndfhs.org.uk/> (changed
  MCH2002)
  Also listed under DURHAM

NOTTINGHAMSHIRE
Mansfield & District FHS
  CONTACT: Miss B E Flintham, 15 Cranmer Grove, Mansfield, Notts.
  NG19 7JR

Nottinghamshire FHS
  CONTACT: Geoff Harrington, 15 Holme Close, Woodborough,
  NOTTINGHAM NG14 6EX
  E-MAILS: tracy.dodds@tesco.net
  WEB-SITE: www.nottsfhs.org.uk <http://www.nottsfhs.org.uk/>

OXFORDSHIRE
Oxfordshire FHS
CONTACT: Mrs J Kennedy, 19 Mavor Close, Woodstock, Oxford
OX20 1YL
E-MAILS: secretary@ofhs.org.uk
WEB-SITE: www.ofhs.org.uk <http://www.ofhs.org.uk/>

RUTLAND
Leicestershire and Rutland FHS
CONTACT: Ray Broad, 11 Spring Lane, Wymondham, Leicestershire
LE14 2AY
E-MAILS: ray.broad@ntlworld.com
WEB-SITE: freepage.genealogy.rootsweb.com/~leicsrut
<http://freepages.genealogy.rootsweb.com/~leicsrut/>
Also listed under LEICESTERSHIRE

SHROPSHIRE
Shropshire FHS
CONTACT: Mrs D Hills, Redhillside, Ludlow Road, Church Stretton,
Shropshire SY6 6AD
E-MAILS: secretary@sfhs.org.uk
WEB-SITE: www.sfhs.org.uk <http://www.sfhs.org.uk>

SOMERSET
Somerset & Dorset FHS
CONTACT: The Secretary, PO Box 4502 Sherborne DT9 6YL
E-MAILS: society@sdfhs.org
WEB-SITE: www.sdfhs.org <http://www.sdfhs.org>
Also listed under DORSET

Weston-super-mare FHS
CONTACT: Kerry James, 32 Marconi Close, Weston Super Mare
BS23 3HH
E-MAILS: kes.jack@virgin.net
WEB-SITE: www.wsmfhs.org.uk <http://www.wsmfhs.org.uk>

Bristol & Avon FHS
CONTACT: Mrs Audrey Lovell, 784 Muller Road, Eastville, Bristol
BS5 6XA
WEB-SITE: www.bafhs.org.uk <http://www.bafhs.org.uk>
Also listed under GLOUCESTERSHIRE

STAFFORDSHIRE
Birmingham & Midland SGH
CONTACT: Mrs Olive Price, 9 Claydon Grove, Yardley Wood,
Birmingham, B14 4NB
E-MAILS: gensec@bmsgh.org
WEB-SITE: www.bmsgh.org <http://www.bmsgh.org/>
Also listed under WARWICKSHIRE and WORCESTERSHIRE

Burntwood FH Group
CONTACT: Mrs P Woodburn, 71 Lawnswood Avenue, Hammerwich,
Burntwood, Staffs WS7 8FZ

SUFFOLK
Felixstowe FHS
CONTACT: Mrs J S Campbell, 7 Victoria Road, Felixstowe, Suffolk
IP11 7PT
WEB-SITE: www.btinternet.com/~woodsbj/ffhs
<http://www.btinternet.com/~woodsbj/ffhs/>

Suffolk FHS
CONTACT: Mrs P Turner, 48 Princethorpe Road, Ipswich IP3 8NX
E-MAILS: jamestrishturner@btinternet.com (changed DEC2001)
WEB-SITE: www.genuki.org.uk/big/eng/SFK/sfhs/sfhs.htm
<http://www.genuki.org.uk/bit/eng/SFK/sfhs/sfhs.htm>

SURREY
East Surrey FHS
CONTACT: Mrs Marion Brackpool, 370 Chipstead Valley Road,
Coulsdon, Surrey CR5 3BF
WEB-SITE: www.eastsurreyfhs.org.uk
<http://www.eastsurreyfhs.org.uk>
Also listed under LONDON (Greater London)

West Surrey FHS
CONTACT: Mrs S McQuire, Deer Dell, Botany Hill, Sands, Farnham,
Surrey GU10 1LZ
E-MAILS: sylviamcq@onetel.net.uk
WEB-SITE: www.surreyweb.org.uk/wsfhs
<http://www.surreyweb.org.uk/wsfhs/>

SUSSEX

Eastbourne & District FHS
> CONTACT: Mrs Sarah Slaughter, 94 Northbourne Road, Eastbourne,
> East Sussex BN22 8QP
> E-MAILS: sarahslaughter@madasafish.com

Hastings & Rother FHS
> CONTACT: Miss Christine Heywood, Flat 22, The Cloisters,
> St Leonards-On-Sea, East Sussex TN37 6JT
> WEB-SITE: www.hrfhs.org.uk <http://www.hrfhs.org.uk>

Sussex FHG
> CONTACT: Mrs J E Chamberlain Hare, 7 Tower View, Manor Park,
> Uckfield, East Sussex TN22 1SB
> E-MAILS: secretary@sfhg.org.uk
> WEB-SITE: www.sfhg.org.uk <http://www.sfhg.org.uk/>

WARWICKSHIRE

Warwickshire FHS
> CONTACT: The Secretary, c/o 7 Mersey Road, Bulkington,
> Warwickshire CV12 9BQ
> E-MAILS: n.wetton@virgin.net
> WEB-SITE: www.wfhs.org.uk <http://www.wfhs.org.uk/>

Birmingham & Midland SGH
> CONTACT: Mrs Olive Price, 9 Claydon Grove, Yardley Wood,
> Birmingham B14 4NB
> E-MAILS: gensec@bmsgh.org
> WEB-SITE: www.bmsgh.org <http://www.bmsgh.org/>
> *Also listed under STAFFORDSHIRE and WORCESTERSHIRE*

Coventry FHS
> CONTACT: Coventry Family History Society, PO Box 2746, Coventry
> CV5 7YD (changed NOV2001)
> WEB-SITE: www.covfhs.org <http://www.covfh.org/> (changed
> JAN2002)

Nuneaton & North Warwickshire FHS
> CONTACT: Leigh Riddell, Gen. Secretary, 14 Amos Avenue,
> Nuneaton, Warwickshire CV10 7BD
> E-MAILS: secretary@nnwfhs.org.uk
> WEB-SITE: www.nnwfhs.org.uk <http://www.nnwfhs.org.uk>

Rugby FHS
    CONTACT: Mr John A Chard, Springfields, Rocheberie Way, RUGBY
    CV22 6EG
    E-MAILS: j.chard@ntlworld.com
    WEB-SITE: www.rugbyfhg.co.uk <http://www.rugbyfhg.co.uk/>
    (added APR2002)

WESTMORLAND
Cumbria FHS
    CONTACT: Mrs M Russell, 32 Granada Road, Denton, Manchester
    M34 2IJ
    WEB-SITE: www.genuki.org.uk/gig/eng/CUL/cumbFHS
    <http://www.genuki.org.uk/big/eng/CUL/cumbFHS/>
    Also listed under CUMBERLAND

WILTSHIRE
Wiltshire FHS
    CONTACT: Secretary, 10 Castle Lane, Devizes, Wilts SN10 1HJ
    WEB-SITE: www.genuki.org.uk/big/eng/WIL/WFHS
    <http://www.genuki.org.uk/big/eng/WIL/WFHS/>

WORCESTERSHIRE
Birmingham & Midland SGH
    CONTACT: Mrs Olive Price, 9 Claydon Grove, Yardley Wood,
    Birmingham B14 4NB
    E-MAILS: gensec@bmsgh.org
    WEB-SITE: www.bmsgh.org <http://www.bmsgh.org/>
    Also listed under STAFFORDSHIRE and WARWICKSHIRE

Malvern FH Group
    CONTACT: Roy Daughtree, D'Haute Rive, 37 Tennyson Drive,
    St James Park, Malvern, Worcs WR14 2TQ
    WEB-SITE: www.mfhg.org.uk <http://www.mfhg.org.uk/> (now back
    on-line MCH2002)

YORKSHIRE
Yorkshire Archaeological Society FH Section
    CONTACT: Miss Lydia Raistrick, c/o YAS, Claremont, 23 Clarendon
    Road, Leeds LS2 9NZ
    E-MAILS: lynda@raistrickl.freeserve.co.uk
    WEB-SITE: www.users.globalnet.co.uk/~gdl/yasfhs.htm
    <http://www.users.globalnet.co.uk/~gdl/yasfhs.htm>

Yorkshire – East Riding
City of York & District FHS
    CONTACT: Mrs Dorothy Croft, 140 Shipton Road, York YO30 5RU
    (changed MCH2002)
    WEB-SITE: www.yorkfamilyhistory.org.uk
    <http://www.yorkfamilyhistory.org.uk/>

East Yorkshire FHS
    CONTACT: Mrs M S Oliver, 12 Carlton Drive, Aldbrough, East Yorks
    HU11 4SF
    WEB-SITE: www.eyfhs.org.uk <http://www.eyfhs.org.uk/>

Yorkshire – North Riding
Cleveland, N. Yorkshire & S. Durham FHS
    CONTACT: Mr A Sampson, 1 Oxgang Close, Redcar, Cleveland TS10
    4ND
    WEB-SITE: website.lineone.net/~pjoiner/cfhs/cfhs.html
    <http://website.lineone.net/~pjoiner/cfhs/cfhs.html>
    Also listed under DURHAM

Yorkshire – West Riding
Barnsley FHS
    CONTACT: Mrs K Wright, 58A High Street, Royston, Barnsley,
    S Yorks S71 4RN
    E-MAILS: kath@barnsleyfhs.freeserve.co.uk
    WEB-SITE: www.barnsleyfhs.freeserve.co.uk
    <http://www.barnsleyfhs.freeserve.co.uk/>

Bradford FHS
    CONTACT: Mr Dennis Flaxington, 2 Leaventhorpe Grove, Thornton,
    Bradford, W. Yorks BD 13 3BN
    E-MAILS: DFlax@aol.com
    WEB-SITE: www.genuki.org.uk/big/eng/YKS/bfhs
    <http://www.genuki.org.uk/big/eng/YKS/bfhs/>

Calderdale FHS (incorporating Halifax & District)
    CONTACT: Mrs M Walker, 61 Gleanings Avenue, Norton Tower,
    Halifax HX2 0NU
    E-MAILS: mail@cfhsweb.co.uk
    WEB-SITE: www.cfhsweb.co.uk <http://www.cfhsweb.co.uk/>

Doncaster & District FHS
CONTACT: Mr J. Staniforth, 125 The Grove, Wheatley Hills,
Doncaster DN2 5SN
E-MAILS: Marton-House@blueyonder.com (changed NOV2001)
WEB-SITE: www.doncasterfhs.freeserve.co.uk
<http://www.doncasterfhs.freeserve.co.uk/>

Huddersfield & District FHS
CONTACT: Mrs Eileen Bass, 292 Thornhills Lane, Clifton, Brighouse,
W. Yorks HD6 4JQ
E-MAILS: secretary@hdfhs.org.uk
WEB-SITE: www.hdfhs.org.uk <http://www.hdfs.org.uk>

Keighley & District FHS
CONTACT: Mrs S Daynes, 2 The Hallowes, Shann Park, Keighley, W.
Yorks BD20 6HY
WEB-SITE: www.ffhs.org.uk/members/keighley.htm
<http://ffhs.org.uk/members/keighley.htm>

Morley & District FH Group
CONTACT: Mrs B Moxon, 26 Wynyard Drive, Morley, Leeds
LS27 9NA
E-MAILS: secretary@morleyfhg.co.uk
WEB-SITE: www.morleyfhg.co.uk <http://morleyfhg.co.uk/>

Pontefract & District FHS
CONTACT: Mrs V Teasdale, 62 Wheatfield Avenue, Oakes,
Huddersfield HD3 4FR
WEB-SITE: freespace.virgin.net/richard.lockwood
<http://freespace.virgin.net/richard.lockwood/>

Ripon, Harrogate & District FHG
CONTACT: Mrs W A Symington, 18 Aspin Drive, Knaresborough,
N. Yorks HG5 8HH
WEB-SITE: www.users.globalnet.co.uk/~gdl/rh1.htm
<http://www.users.globalnet.co.uk/~gdl/rh1.htm>

Rotherham FHS (new member JAN2001)
CONTACT: Ron Bye, 12 Hall Grove, Moorgate, Rotherham, S. Yorks
S60 2BS
E-MAILS: ronbye@hotmail.com
WEB-SITE: www.rotherhamfhs.f9.co.uk
<http://www.rotherhamfhs.f9.co.uk>

Sheffield & District FHS
   CONTACT: Mrs J Pitchforth, 10 Hallam Grange Road, Sheffield
   S10 4BJ
   E-MAILS: secretary@sheffieldfhs.org.uk
   WEB-SITE: www.sheffieldfhs.org.uk
   <http://www.sheffieldfhs.org.uk>

Wakefield & District FHS
   CONTACT: Mrs Jean Howgate, 11 Waterton Close, Walton,
   Wakefield, W. Yorks WF2 6JT
   E-MAILS: general.secretary@virgin.net
   WEB-SITE: www.wdfhs.co.uk <http://www.wdfhs.co.uk/> (changed
   NOV2001)

Wharfedale FHG
   CONTACT: Mrs Susan Hartley, 1 West View Court, Yeadon, Leeds
   LS19 7HX
   WEB-SITE: www.users.globalnet.co.uk/~gdl/wfhg1.htm
   <http://www.users.globalnet.co.uk/~gdl/wfhg1.htm>

Appendix 3

GENEALOGY AND FAMILY HISTORY BIBLIOGRAPHY

General

A Bevan (ed.), *Tracing Your Ancestors in the Public Record Office* (PRO, 5th revised edn 1999)

S Colwell, *Dictionary of Genealogy Sources in the Public Record Office* (London, 1992)

J Foster and J Sheppard, *British Archives, A Guide to Archive Resources in the United Kingdom* (London, 3rd edn 1995)

Gallery One: Naming Names and Tracing Places

E Churchill (ed.), *Census Copies and Indexes in the Library of the Society of Genealogists* (Society of Genealogists, 3rd edn 1997)

J Gibson and E Churchill, *The Hearth Tax Returns, other later Stuart Tax Lists, and the Association Oath Rolls* (FFHS, 2nd edn 1996)

J Gibson, *Probate jurisdictions: Where to look for wills* (FFHS, 5th edn 2002)

J Gibson and A Dell, *Tudor and Stuart Muster Rolls, A Directory of holdings in the British Isles* (FFHS, 1991)

J Gibson and E Hampson, *Census Returns, 1841–1891, in Microform, A Directory to Local Holdings in Great Britain and Ireland; Channel Islands; Isle of Man* (FFHS, 6th edn 1997)

J Gibson and E Hampson, *Marriage and Census Indexes for Family Historians* (FFHS, 7th edn 1998)

J Gibson and M Medlycott, *Local census listings, 1522–1930, holdings in the British Isles* (FFHS, 3rd edn 1997)

J Gibson and M Medlycott, *Militia Lists and Musters, 1757–1876* (FFHS, 3rd edn 1994)

J S W Gibson, M Medlycott and D Mills, *Land and Window Tax Assessments, 1690–1950* (FFHS, 2nd edn 1998)

J Gibson and P Peskett, *Record Offices; How to find them* (FFHS, 8th edn 1998)

Guildhall Library, *The British Overseas* (Guildhall Library, 3rd, revised edn 1995)

D Hawgood, *Family Search on the Internet* (FFHS, 1999)

M Herber, *Clandestine marriages in the Chapel and Rules of the Fleet, 1680–1754, 2 vols* (London, 1998–99)

E Higgs, *A Clearer Sense of the Census: the Manuscript Returns for England and Wales, 1801–1901* (HMSO, 1996)

R Hoyle, *Tudor Taxation Records, A Guide for Users* (PRO, 1994)

C Humphery-Smith, *The Phillimore Atlas and Index of Parish Registers* (Chichester, 2nd edn 1995)

M Jurkowski, C L Smith and D Crook, *Lay Taxes in England and Wales 1188–1688* (PRO, 1998)

F Leeson, *A Guide to the Records of the British State Tontines and Life Annuities of the 17th and 18th Centuries* (Shalfleet Manor, 1968)

S Lumas, *Making Use of the Census* (PRO, 3rd edn 1997)

R Milward, *A Glossary of Household, Family and Trade Terms from Probate Inventories* (Derbyshire Record Office, 3rd edn 1993)

I Mortimer (ed.), *Record Repositories in Great Britain* (PRO, 11th edn 1999)

L Munby, *Reading Tudor and Stuart Handwriting* (British Association for Local History, 1988)

M Nissel, *People Count, A History of the General Register Office* (HMSO, 1987)

M Scott, *Prerogative Court of Canterbury Wills and Other Probate Records* (PRO, 1997)

D. Shorney, *Protestant Nonconformity and Roman Catholicism, A guide to sources in the Public Record Office* (PRO, 1996)

Gallery Two: People at work

D Hawkings, *Railway ancestors* (Stroud, 1995)

J Herlithy, *The Royal Irish Constabulary* (Dublin, 1997)

T Richards, *Was your grandfather a railwayman?* (FFHS, 3rd edn 1995)

W Spencer, *Air Force Records for Family Historians* (PRO, 2000)

G Thomas, *Records of the Royal Marines* (PRO 1994)

Titanic 14th–15th April 1912, The Official Story (PRO document pack, 1997)

Gallery Three: The Army and Navy

Battlefront: 1st July 1916: The first day of the Somme (PRO document pack, 1996)

E W Bell, *Soldiers Killed on the First Day of the Somme* (Bolton, 1977)

T Cross, *The Lost Voices of World War I, An International Anthology of Writers, Poets and Playwrights* (London, 1988)

S Fowler and W Spencer, *Army Records for Family Historians* (PRO, 2nd edn 1998)

S Fowler, W Spencer and S Tamblin, *Army Service Records of the First World War* (PRO, 2nd edn 1997)

C Hobson, *Airmen Died in the Great War 1914–1918: the roll of honour of the British and Commonwealth Air Services of the First World War* (Polstead, 1995)

N Holding, revised and updated by I Swinnerton, *The Location of British Army Records, 1914–1918* (FFHS, 4th edn 1999)

N Holding, *More Sources of World War I Ancestry* (FFHS, 3rd edn 1998)

N Holding, *World War I Army Ancestry* (FFHS 3rd edn 1997)

R Holmes, *The Western Front* (London, 1999)

Marquis de Ruvigny, *The Roll of Honour: a biographical record of members of His Majesty's Naval and Military Forces who fell in the Great War* (2 vols, London 1986 reprint)

G Oram and J Putkowski, *Death sentences passed by military courts of the British Army, 1914–1924* (London, 1988)

J Putkowski, *British Army mutineers, 1914–1922* (London, 1998)

N A M Rodger, *Naval Records for Family Historians* (PRO, 1998)

C K Schaefer, *The Great War, A Guide to The Service Records of All The World's Fighting Men and Volunteers* (Baltimore, 1998)

J Silkin, *The Penguin Book of First World War Poetry* (London, 2nd edn 1996)

K Smith, C T Watts and M J Watts, *Records of Merchant Shipping and Seamen* (PRO, 1998) *Soldiers Died in the Great War, 1914–19* (CD-ROM, Heathfield, 1998)

The Times Diary and Index of the War, 1914–18 (Polstead, 1985)

H Williamson, *A Dictionary of Great War Abbreviations* (Harwich, 1996)

T and S Wise, *A Guide to Military Museums and other places of military interest* (Knighton, 9th revised edn 1999)

Gallery Four: Migrant Ancestors

P W Coldham, *American Loyalist Claims, Audit Office Series 13, bundles 1–35, and 37* (Baltimore, 1980)

P W Coldham, *American Wills and Administrations in the Prerogative Court of Canterbury, 1610–1857* (Baltimore, 1989)

P W Coldham, *American Wills proved in London, 1611–1775* (Baltimore, 1992)

P W Coldham, *The Complete Book of Emigrants, 1607–1776* (4 vols, Baltimore, 1987–1993)

P W Filby and M K Meyer, ed., *Passenger and Immigration Lists Index* (Detroit, 1981, with annual Supplements 1982–   )

J Gibson and C Rogers, *Poor Law Union Records, 3 parts* (FFHS, 1993–97)

J Gibson and F A Youngs, Jr, *Poor Law Union Records: 4 Gazeteer of England and Wales* (FFHS, 1993)

G Grannum, *Tracing Your West Indian Ancestors, Sources in the Public Record Office* (PRO, 1995)

R Kershaw and M Pearsall, *Immigrants and Aliens, A guide to sources* (PRO, 2000)

Gallery Five: Ancestors and the Law

M Cale, *Law and Society, An Introduction to Sources for Criminal and Legal History from 1800* (PRO, 1996)

C R Cheney, *Handbook of Dates for Students of English History* (Royal Historical Society, 1945, reprinted with corrections 1991)

P. W Coldham, *Complete Book of Emigrants in Bondage, 1614–1775* (Baltimore, 1987, Supplement 1992)

J Gibson and C Rogers, *Coroners' Records in England and Wales* (FFHS, 2nd edn 1997)

D T Hawkings, *Bound for Australia* (Chichester, 1987)

D T Hawkings, *Criminal Ancestors, A Guide to Historical Criminal Records in England and Wales* (Stroud, 1992)

H Horwitz, *Chancery Equity Records and Proceedings 1600–1800* (PRO, 1998)

W P W Phillimore and E A Fry, An Index to Changes of Name ... 1760–1901 (London, 1905, reprinted 1986)

H Sharp, *How to Use the Bernau Index* (London, 1996)

British readers should check ***amazon.co.uk*** first (author or title search) for the following which give the amazon.com web page.

- *Ancestral Trails: The Complete Guide to British Genealogy and Family History*
 <http://www.amazon.com/exec/obidos/ISBN=0806315415/ markcyndisgenealA/>
 Mark D. Herber.

- *Atlas of British Surnames: With 154 Maps of Selected Surnames*
 <http://www.amazon.com/exec/obidos/ISBN=0814322530/ markcyndisgenealA/>
 Gabriel Ward Lasker.

- *Audacious Women: Early British Mormon Immigrants*
 <http://www.amazon.com/exec/obidos/ISBN=1560850663/ markcyndisgenealA/>
 Rebecca Batholomew.

- *Bishops' Transcripts and Marriage Licenses, Bonds and Allegations: A Guide to Their Locations and Indexes*
  <http://www.amazon.com/exec/obidos/ISBN=0806313560/ markcyndisgenealA/>
  J S Gibson.

- *The British insurance business: a guide to its history & records*
  <http://www.amazon.com/exec/obidos/ISBN=1850754519/ markcyndisgenealA/>
  H A L Cockerell.

- *Cambridge University Alumni: 1261–1900*
  <http://www.amazon.com/exec/obidos/ISBN=1888486767/ markcyndisgenealA/>
  A CD-ROM by Ancestry.

- Chapman Rocord Cameos
  <http://www.genuki.org.uk/big/Chapman. html>
  A series of books by Colin R. Chapman, noted British genealogist.

- *The Dictionary of Genealogy*
  <http://www.amazon.com/exec/obidos/ISBN=0713648597/ markcyndisgenealA/>
  Terrick H. Fitzhugh.

- *Empty Cradles*
  <http://www.amazon.com/exec/obidos/ISBN=055214164X/ markcyndisgenealA/>
  Margaret Humphreys.

- *English Handwriting, 1400–1650: An Introductory Manual*
  <http://www.amazon.com/exec/obidos/ISBN=0866980865/ markcyndisgenealA/>
  Jean F Preston.

- *Family Names and Family History*
  <http://www.amazon.co.uk/exec/obidos/ASIN/1852852550/ markandcyndisgen/>
  David Hey.

◆ *A Genealogist's Guide to Discovering Your English Ancestors*
  <http://www.amazon.com/exec/obidos/ISBN=1558705368/
  markcyndisgenealA/>
  by Paul Milner & Linda Jonas. This is an excellent beginner's book
  on UK genealogy particularly for those outside of the United
  Kingdom.

◆ *The Genealogist's Internet*
  <http://www.amazon.co.uk/exec/obidos/ASIN/1903365163/
  markandcyndisgen>
  Peter Christian.

◆ *A Guide to the Historical Records of British Banking*
  <http://www.amazon.com/exec/obidos/ISBN=0312353030/
  markcyndisgenealA/>
  L S Pressnell.

◆ *The Hearth Tax, Other Later Stuart Tax Lists, and the Association*
  Oath Rolls
  <http://www.amazon.com/exec/obidos/ISBN=0806312890/
  markcyndisgenealA/>
  Jeremy Gibson.

◆ *Huguenots in Britain and Their French Background 1550–1800*
  <http://www.amazon.com/exec/obidos/ISBN=0389207055/
  markcyndisgenealA/>
  Irene Scouloudi.

◆ *Kings, Queens, Bones and Bastards: Who's Who in the English*
  Monarchy from Egbert to Elizabeth II
  <http://www.amazon.com/exec/obidos/ISBN=0750917415/
  markcyndisgenealA/>
  David Hilliam.

◆ *The Kings and Queens of England*
  <http://www.amazon.com/exec/obidos/ISBN=0821222554/
  markcyndisgenealA/>
  Nicholas Best.

◆ *Making Use of the Census*
  <http://www.amazon.com/exec/obidos/ISBN=187316243X/
  markcyndisgenealA/>
  Susan Lumas.

- *The Mammoth Book of British Kings & Queens*
  <http://www.amazon.com/exec/obidos/ISBN=0786706929/
  markcyndisgenealA/>
  Mike Ashley.

- *Marriage, Census, and Other Indexes for Family Historians*
  <http://www.amazon.com/exec/obidos/ISBN=080631358/
  markcyndisgenealA/>
  Jeremy Gibson & Elizabeth Hampson.

- *Never Been Here Before?: A Genealogists' Guide to the Family*
  Records Centre
  <http://www.amazon.com/exec/obidos/ISBN=1873162413/
  markcyndisgenealA/>
  Jane Cox.

- *The Oxford Companion to Local and Family History*
  <http://www.amazon.com/exec/obidos/ISBN=0192116886/
  markcyndisgenealA/>
  David Hey.

- *The Oxford Guide to Family History*
  <http://www.amazon.com/exec/obidos/ISBN=0198691777/
  markcyndisgenealA/>
  David Hey.

- *The Oxford Illustrated History of the British Monarchy*
  <http://www.amazon.com/exec/obidos/ISBN=019288073X/
  markcyndisgenealA/>
  Ralph Alan Griffiths.

- *The Plantagenet Ancestry*
  <http://www.amazon.com/exec/obidos/ISBN=0806303301/
  markcyndisgenealA/>
  W H Turton.

- *Poll Books C. 1696–1872*
  <http://www.amazon.com/exec/obidos/ISBN=9991650253/
  markcyndisgenealA/>
  Jeremy Gibson.

- *Protestant Non-Conformity & Roman Catholicism – PRO Readers' Guide No. 13*
  <http://www.amazon.com/exec/obidos/ISBN=1873162278/markcyndisgenealA/>
  David Shorney.

- *Reader's Digest Explore Your Family's Past*
  <http://www.amazon.co.uk/exec/obidos/ASIN/0276424468/markandcyndisgen>
  Reader's Digest.

- *Tracing the History of Villages*
  <http://www.amazon.co.uk/exec/obidos/ASIN/1853067121/markandcyndisgen>
  Trevor Yorke.

- *Tracing Your Ancestors in the Public Record Office*
  <http://www.amazon.com/exec/obidos/ISBN=1873162618/markcyndisgenealA/>
  Amanda Bevan.

- *Was your grandfather a railwayman?*
  <http://www.amazon.com/exec/obidos/ISBN=0907099807/markcyndisgenealA/>
  Tom Richards.

- *Who Lies Where: A Guide to Famous Graves*
  <http://www.amazon.com/exec/obidos/ISBN=1857022580/markcyndisgenealA/>
  Michael Kerrigan.

Appendix 4

USEFUL WEBSITES AND ADDRESSES

Borthwick Institute of Historical Research
St Anthony's Hall
Peasholme Green
York YO1 7PW
Tel 01904 642315
www.york.ac.uk/inst/bihr

College of Arms
Queen Victoria Street
London EC4V 4BT
http://www.cwgc.org

Commonwealth War Graves Commission
2 Marlow Road
Maidenhead
Berkshire SL6 7DX
Tel 01628 634221
email: mailto:cwgc@dial.pipex.com

Court Funds Division
www.open.gov/cwgc/cwgchome.htm

Public Trust House
22 Kingsway
London WC2B 6LE
http://www.earl.org.uk/familia/

Familia (Family History Resources in Public Libraries in Britain and
Ireland)
http://www.earl.org.uk/familia/
http://www.pro.gov.uk

Family Records Centre (Public Record Office)
http://www.pro.gov.uk   http://www.ons.gov.uk

Family Records Centre (Office for National Statistics)
http://www.ons.gov.uk%20%20
1 Myddleton Street
London EC1R 1UW
Tel 020 8392 5300 (general enquiries)
020 7533 6438 (Scotlink)
0151 471 4800 (certificate enquiries)
email: certificate.service@ons.gov.uk
see also General Register Office/Office for National Statistics

Federation of Family History Societies
PO BOX 2425
COVENTRY
CV5 6YX
email: info@ffhs.org.uk
http://www.ffhs.org.uk

Friends Library
Friends House
173–177 Euston Road
London NW1 2BJ
http://www.lds.org/

Genealogical Society of Utah
Church of Jesus Christ of Latter-day Saints (home)
http://www.lds.org/
http://www.familysearch.org/

Genealogical Society of Utah
Church of Jesus Christ of Latter-day Saints (family search)
http://www.familysearch.org/
185 Penns Lane
Sutton Coldfield
West Midlands B76 1JU
Tel 0121 384 2028
http://www.ons.gov.uk

General Register Office/Office for National Statistics
http://www.ons.gov.uk
PO Box 2
Southport
Merseyside PR8 2JD
Tel 0151 471 4800 (certificate enquiries)
email: certificate.service@ons.gov.uk
http://www.ons.gov.uk

General Register Office (Ireland)
Joyce House
8–11 Lombard Street
East Dublin 2
Tel 0035 31 6711000
http://www.groireland.ie

General Register Office (Northern Ireland)
Oxford House
49–55 Chichester Street
Belfast BT1 4HL
Tel 01232 252021
http://www.open.gov.uk/gros/
http://www.nics.gov.uk/nisra/gro

General Register Office (Scotland)
(home) http://www.open.gov.uk/gros/
http://www.origins.net/GRO/

General Register Office (Scotland) (origins)
Edinburgh EH1 3YT
Tel 0131 334 0380
email: nrh.gros@gtnet.gov.uk
http://www.origins.net/GRO/New Register House

Guildhall Library
Aldermanbury
London EC2P 2EJ
http://www.hmc.gov.uk/archon/

Historical Manuscripts Commission (lists record repositories)
http://www.hmc.gov.uk/archon/

House of Lords Record Office
London SW1A 0PW
http://www.iwm.org.uk

Imperial War Museum
Lambeth Road
London SE1 6HZ
Tel 020 7416 5221
email: docs@iwm.org.uk
http://www.iwm.org.uk

Lambeth Palace Library
London SE1 7JU
Tel 020 7898 1400
http://www.arbeia.demon.co.uk/museums/

Military Museums
http://www.arbeia.demon.co.uk/museums/
http://www.mod.uk/   http://www.mod.uk/

Ministry of Defence
CS (R) 2b Bourne Avenue
Hayes
Middlesex UB3 1RF
http://www.nationalarchives.ie/
http://www.mod.uk/

National Archives of Ireland
Bishop Street
Dublin 8
Tel 00 35 31 4072300
email: mail@nationalarchives.ie
http://www.nationalarchives.ie/

National Archives of Scotland
HM General Register House
2 Princes Street
Edinburgh EH1 3YY
Tel 0131 535 1314
email: research@nas.gov.uk

National Inventory of War Memorials
Imperial War Museum
Lambeth Road
London SE1 6HZ
Tel 0120 7416 5353
email: memorials@iwm.org.uk
http://www.llgc.org.uk

National Library of Wales
Aberystwyth
Dyfed SY23 3BU
Tel 01970 632800
email: ymh.lc@llgc.org.uk
http://www.bl.uk/collections/oriental
http://www.llgc.org.uk/

Oriental and India Office Collections
http://www.bl.uk/collections/oriental

British Library
96 Euston Road
London NW1 2DB
Tel 020 7412 7513
email: oic-enquiries@bl.uk

Probate Search Room
Principal Registry of the Family Division
42–49 High Holborn
London WC1V 6NP
Tel 020 7947 6000 (probate and divorce)
http://proni.nics.gov.uk/

Public Record Office of Northern Ireland
66 Balmoral Avenue
Belfast BT9 6NY
Tel 028 9025 5905
email: proni@nics.gov.uk
http:/proni.nics.gov.uk/

Registry of Shipping and Seamen
Anchor House
Cheviot Close
Parc Ty Glas
Llanishen
Cardiff CF4 5JA

Royal Courts of Justice
Room 8
Strand
London WC2A 2LL
http://www.sog.org.uk/

Society of Genealogists
14 Charterhouse Buildings
Goswell Road
London EC1M 7BA
Tel 020 7251 8799
email: library@sog.org.uk
http://www.sog.org.uk/

Appendix 5

FAMILY HISTORY AND GENEALOGY GLOSSARY OF TERMS

abstract
abbreviated transcription of a document or record that includes the date of the record, every name appearing therein, the relationship (if stated) of each person named and their description (i.e., witness, executor, bondsman, son, widow, etc.), and if they signed with their signature or mark.

ad litem
legal term meaning *in this case only*. For Example, 'George Thomas, duly appointed by the court, may administer ad litem the settlement of the estate of Joseph Thomas, deceased.'

adm. (abbreviation)
administrator, administration.

admin. (abbreviation)
administrator, administration.

admin. (abbreviation)
letters of administration

administration
a court action used to settle the estate of a person who died without leaving a will, or a person who left a will that the court disallowed, or where the executor appointed by the deceased refuses to serve in that capacity.

affidavit
a written or oral statement made under oath.

ahnentafel
ancestor table, tabulates the ancestry of one individual by generation in text rather than pedigree chart format. A comprehensive ahnentafel gives more than the individual's name, date and place of birth, christening, marriage, death and burial. It should give biographical and historical commentary for each person listed, as well as footnotes citing the source documents used to prove what is stated.

ahnentafel number
the unique number assigned to each position in an ancestor table is called an ahnentafel number. Number one designates the person in the first generation. Numbers two and three designate the parents of number one and the second generation. Numbers four through seven

designate the grandparents of person number one and the third generation. As the ahnentafel extends by generation, the number of persons doubles.

a.k.a.

also known as; alias.

alien

a citizen of another country

ancestor

a person from whom you descend; grandparents, great-grandparents, 2nd great-grandparents (also called great great-grandparents), 3rd great-grandparents, etc.; direct-line ancestor; forefather; forebear.

Ancestral File

a genealogical system developed by the Family History Department of the Church of Jesus Christ of Latter-day Saints (LDS Church), links individuals to ancestors in pedigree, family group, and descendant formats. It contains genealogical information about millions of people from many nations.

ancestry

denotes all of your ancestors from your parents as far back as they are traceable. Estimates suggest that everyone has approximately 65,000 *traceable ancestors*, meaning ancestors whose existence can be documented in surviving records.

anon. (abbreviation)

anonymous

annotation

interpretations, explanation, clarification, definition, or supplement. Many types of genealogical presentations contain statements, record sources, documents, conclusions, or other historical information that require an annotation. Generally, annotations appear in footnotes, end-notes, or in the text itself. Genealogical software provides a field for documentation, comments, notes, and analysis. Genealogists use annotations to explain discrepancies between two or more documents, to add information from another source to support a statement or conclusion made in a different record, and other situations difficult to interpret.

appr. (abbreviation)

appraisal; appraisement.

assignment

grant of property or a legal right, benefit, or privilege to another person.

authenticate

prove a document is not a forgery.

b. (abbreviation)
> born

B (abbreviation)
> Black, indicating race.

banns
> public announcement of an intended marriage, generally made in church.

bapt. (abbreviation)
> baptized.

base-born
> a base-born individual was an illegitimate child.

bastard
> a bastard is an illegitimate child.

biographies
> a biography is a book written about a particular individual. You can also find compiled biographies, which are books that contain short biographies of many different people. A compiled biography normally is about a specific group of people. For example, you can find compiled biographies about individuals who were involved in a particular profession or who lived in a particular area. You can usually find the following information in a biography: occupation, accomplishments, affiliations, and family information.

birth records
> a birth record contains information about the birth of an individual. On a birth record, you can usually find the mother's full maiden name and the father's full name, the name of the baby, the date of the birth, and the county where the birth took place. Many birth records include other information, such as the birthplace of the baby's parents, the addresses of the parents, the number of children that the parents have, and the race of the parents, and the parents' occupations.

bef. (abbreviation)
> before.

bequeath
> term appearing in a will meaning to leave or give property as specified therein to another person or organization.

bet. (abbreviation)
> between.

bibliography
> list of writings relating to a specific subject, some of which are annotated. A bibliographic citation describes and identifies the author, edition, date of issue, publisher, and typography of a book or other written material. Generally, bibliographies appear at the end of a publication to indicate the sources used by the author or to suggest

titles for additional reading. Bibliographic citations appear in footnotes and end-notes to document the source of a statement made in the body of a writing.

bond

writen, binding agreement to perform as specified. Many types of bonds have existed for centuries and appear in marriage, land and court records used by genealogists. Historically, laws required administrators and executors of estates, grooms alone or with others, and guardians of minors to post bonds. It is not unusual to discover that a bondsman was related to someone involved in the action before the court. If a bondsman failed to perform, the court may have demanded payment of a specified sum as a penalty.

bounds

pertaining to measuring natural or man-made features on the land.

bounty land

land promised as an inducement for enlistment or payment for military services. A central government did not exist when the Revolutionary War began, nor did a treasury. Land, the greatest asset the new nation possessed, was used to induce enlistment and as payment for military services. Those authorized to bounty land received a Bounty Land Warrant from the newly formed government after the war.

bp. (abbreviation)

baptized.

bpt. (abbreviation)

baptized.

bro. (abbreviation)

brother.

bu. (abbreviation)

buried.

bur. (abbreviation)

buried.

c., ca. (abbreviation)

about or around, from the Latin word *circa*.

cem. (abbreviation)

cemetery.

cemetery records

cemetery caretakers usually keep records of the names and death dates of those buried, as well as maps of the grave sites. They may also keep more detailed records, including the names of the deceased's relatives. In addition to these paper records, you will find tombstones. Tombstrones can provide information such as birth and death dates and the names of other family members.

census records

a census is an official enumeration of the population in a particular area. In addition to counting the inhabitants of an area, the census generally collects other vital information, such as names, ages, citizenship status, and ethnic background. The United States government began collecting census data in 1790, and has done so every 10 years since that date. Selected states have also conducted their own censuses over the years.

chr. (abbreviation)

christened.

Christian name

names other than a person's last name.

church records

church records are the formal documents that churches have kept about their congregations through the years. Churches normally record information about christenings, baptisms, marriages, and burials. The type of information you will find in the records are the name(s) of the individual(s) involved, the date of the event, the location of the event, and the clergyman's name. You may find additional information, such as parents' names (father's full name and mother's maiden name), the names of witnesses to an event, and the individual's (or family's) place of residence.

civ. (abbreviation)

civil.

civil law

laws concerned with civil or private rights and remedies, as contrasted with criminal law; body of law established by a nation, commonwealth, county or city, also called municipal law.

codicil

supplement or addition to a will; not intended to replace an entire will.

collateral line

line of descent connecting persons who share a common ancestor, but are related through an aunt, uncle, cousin, nephew, etc.

conf. (abbreviation)

confirmed.

consanguinity

the degree of relationship between persons who descend from a common ancestor. A father and son are related by lineal consanguinity, uncle and nephew by collateral sanguinity.

comm. (abbreviation)

communion, communicant.

common ancestor

person through whom two or more persons claim descent or lineage.

communicant

person receiving communion in a religious ceremony or service.

confederacy

Confederate States of America; group of southern states that seceded from the United States from 1860–1865.

consort

wife, husband, spouse, mate, companion.

conveyance

legal document by which the title to property is transferred; warrant; patent; deed.

cousin

child of an aunt or uncle; in earlier times a kinsman, close relative, or friend.

CW

Civil War, War of the Rebellion, War between the States, 1861–1865.

d. (abbreviation)

died.

dau. (abbreviation)

daughter.

daughter-in-law

a daughter-in-law is the wife of an individual's son. Daughter-in-law also used to mean 'step-daughter'.

dec'd. (abbreviation)

deceased.

deceased

commonly written 'the deceased' meaning someone who has died.

descendant

your descendants are your children, grandchildren, great-grandchildren, and so on – anyone to whom you are an ancestor.

declaration of intention

a declaration of intention is a document filed by an alien who intended to become a United States citizen. It could also be a declaration filed by a couple in a local court, indicating their intention to marry.

deed

document transferring ownership and title of property or any other formal declaration of legal intent.

devise

gift or real property by last will and testament of the donor.

devisee

person receiving land or real property in a last will and testament.

devisor
>person giving land or real property in a last will and testament.

direct line
>line of descent traced through persons who are related to one another as a child and parent.

directories
>directories come in all types: city, telephone, county, regional, professional, religious, post office, street, ethnic, and school. The directories you search will depend on the type of information you know about the individual. The information that you can find in a directory depends on the type of directory. For example, city directories normally list names and addresses. In some city directories you can also find information such as children's names, marriage dates, death dates, and birth dates. Other types of directories may provide you with even more interesting information about your ancestors. For instance, a church directory may tell you about an individual's involvement in church activities, professional directories may give you insight into your ancestor's professional life, and club directories may contain information about your ancestor's involvement in social activities.

dissenter
>name given to a person who refused to belong to the established Church of England.

div. (abbreviation)
>divorced.

double date
>the practice of writing double dates resulted from switching from the Julian to the Gregorian calendar, and also from the fact that not all countries and people accepted the new calendar at the same time.

dowager
>widow holding property or a title received from her deceased husband; title given in England to widows or princes, dukes, earls, and other noblemen.

dower
>legal provision of real estate and support made to the widow for her lifetime from a husband's estate.

download
>downloading is electronically extracting files from a network or bulletin board system for use on your own computer. Many bulletin board systems with genealogy sections have files that you can download.

dowry [*also* **dowery**]
>land, money, goods, or personal property brought by a bride to her husband in marriage.

emancipated

freed from slavery; freed from parents' control; of legal age.

emigrant

person leaving one country to reside in another country.

emigration

emigration is when an individual leaves their home country to live in another country.

entail

to entail is to restrict the inheritance of land to a specific group of heirs, such as an individual's sons.

enumeration

list of people, as in a census.

estate

assets and liabilities of a decedent, including land, personal belongings and debts.

et al

'and others'.

et ux

'and wife'.

evidence

any kind of proof, such as testimony, documents, records, certificates, material objects, etc.

exec. (abbreviation)

executor.

exor. (abbreviation)

executor.

exox. (abbreviation)

executrix.

executor

male appointed by a testator to carry out the directions and requests in his or her will, and to dispose of the property according to the testamentary provisions after his or her death.

executrix

female appointed by a testator to carry out the directions and requests in his or her will, and to dispose of the property according to the testamentary provisions after his or her death.

fam. (abbreviation)

family.

family group sheet

a family group sheet is a form which presents genealogical information about a nuclear family – a husband, a wife, and their children. A family group sheet usually includes birth dates and places, death dates and places, and marriage dates and places. Family Tree

Maker for Windows can help you create family group sheets for your family.

family pedigrees

in general, family pedigrees refer to family group sheets that are linked in a computer system. When you access an individual's family group sheet in a linked pedigree, you also access all of the records that are linked to that individual.

family histories/genealogies

family histories and genealogies are books which detail the basic genealogical facts about one or more generations of a particular family.

FamilySearch

you can find FamilySearch computers at the Family History Library of the Church of Jesus Christ of Latter-day Saints or at one of the branch Family History Centres. The FamilySearch computer contains several databases of information: the Social Security Death Index, the Military Index, the Ancestral File, and the International Genealogical Index. You can use these resources to search for information about your family members on the computer. You can also use the FamilySearch computer to look up items in the Family History Library Catalogue. Because of the popularity of the FamilySearch computer, many Family History Centres requre you to sign up for a time slot in advance. FamilySearch is also now available on the internet through the web site of the LDS Church.

fee simple

an inheritance having no limitations or conditions in its use.

feme

female, woman, or wife.

feme sole

unmarried woman or a married woman with property independent of her husband.

fortnight

two weeks.

FR (abbreviation)

family register.

freedman

male released from slavery; emancipated person.

freeman

male of legal age with the right to vote, own land and practise a trade.

free man of colour

Black man who was free from birth or later in life.

full age

age of majority; legal age; adult (legal age varied according to place and current law).

gazetteer

a gazetteer is a book which alphabetically names and describes the places in a specific area. For example, a gazetteer of a county would name and describe all of the towns, lakes, rivers, and mountains in the county.

gdn. (abbreviation)

guardian.

GEDCOM Database

GEnealogy **D**ata **COM**munications, a standardized format for genealogy databases that allows the exchange of data among different software programs and operating systems.

genealogy

study of one's ancestry; summary history or table of a person's ancestry.

good brother

brother-in-law.

good sister

sister-in-law.

good son

son-in-law.

grandam

grandmother.

grantee

person purchasing, buying or receiving property.

grantee index

master index of persons purchasing, buying or receiving property.

grantor

person selling, granting, transferring or conveying property.

grantor index

master index of persons selling, granting, transferring or conveying property.

grdn. (abbreviation)

guardian

guardian

person lawfully appointed to care for a minor, invalid or incompetent person and their interests, such as education, property management and investments.

heir

person who succeeds, by the rules of law, to an estate upon the death of an ancestor; one with rights to inherit an estate.

heir apparent

by law a person whose right of inheritance is established, provided he or she outlives the ancestor. *See also* primogeniture.

holographic will
a holographic or olographic will is handwritten and signed by the individual to whom the will belongs.

homestead
a homestead usually is a home on land obtained from the United States government. Part of the agreement between the individual and the government was that the individual had to live on the land and make improvements to it, such as adding buildings and clearing fields.

hon. (abbreviation)
honourable.

husb. (abbreviation)
husband.

illegitimate
child born to a woman who is not married to the father.

immigrant
person moving into a country from another country.

immigration
immigration is when an individual goes into a new country to live.

imp. (abbreviation)
imported.

indentured servant
person who is bound into the service of another person for a specified period, usually seven years in the 18th and 19th centuries to pay for passage to another country.

index
in genealogical terms, an index is an alphabetical list of names that were taken from a particular set of records. For example, a census record index lists the names of individuals that are found in a particular set of census records. Indices mostly come in book form, but you can also find them on CD-ROM, microfilm, and microfiche.

inf. (abbreviation)
infantry.

infant
person under legal age.

inhab. (abbreviation)
inhabitant; inhabited.

in loco parentis
in place of the parent or parents.

instant (or **inst.**)
of this month.

International Genealogical Index (IGI)
the International Genealogical Index (IGI) is one of the resources of the Family History Library of the Church of Jesus Christ of Latter-

day Saints. Containing approximately 250 million names, it is an index of people's names that were either submitted to the church, or were extracted from records that the church has microfilmed over the years. You can use the IGI to locate information about your ancestors.

intestate

used to denote a person who died without leaving a will.

inventory

an inventory is a legal list of all the property in a deceased person's estate. The executor of the will is requred to make an inventory.

issue

children, descendants, offspring.

jno. (abbreviation)

John or Johannes.

joiner

carpenter who does finish work.

jud. (abbreviation)

judicial.

Julian Calendar

calendar named for Julius Caesar and used from 45 B.C. to 1582, called the 'Old Style' calendar; replaced by the Gregorian calendar.

junr. (abbreviation)

junior.

juvenis

juvenile, minor, under legal age.

knave

servant boy.

knt. (abbreviation)

knight.

land records

land records are deeds – proof that a piece of land is owned by a particular individual. The information you receive from the records will vary, but you will at least get a name, the location of the property, and the period of ownership.

late

denoting someone who is deceased, i.e., the late John Thomas.

legacy

property or money bequeathed to someone in a will.

legatee

someone who inherits money or property from a person who left a will.

lessee

person leasing property from an owner.

lessor
> owner leasing property to a tenant.

Letters Testamentary
> court document allowing the executor named in a will to carry out his or her duties.

liber
> book of public records.

lic. (abbreviation)
> license.

lien
> claim placed on property by a person who is owed money.

life estate
> use interest in property until death.

lineage
> direct line of descent from an ancestor; ancestry; progeny.

lis pendens
> notices of suits pending litigation, usually in matters concerning land.

litigant
> person involved in a lawsuit.

liv. (abbreviation)
> living.

local history
> a local history is usually a book about a particular town or county. Local histories were quite popular in the late 19th century. While they often give the history of the development of the area, they usually also include some information about the important families that lived there.

loyalist
> colonist who supported the British during the American Revolution; Tory.

Ltd. (abbreviation)
> limited.

m. (abbreviation)
> married.

md. (abbreviation)
> married.

maiden name
> a woman's last name prior to marriage.

major
> legal age.

majores
> ancestors.

majority
> legal age.

manse
parsonage; enough land to support a family.

manumission
manumission is the act of being released from slavery or servitude.

manuscript
manuscripts are usually unpublished family histories or collections of family papers. Depending on what the manuscript contains, you may be able to find all kinds of family information. Generally, you will find more than just names, birth dates, and death dates.

marita
married woman, wife.

maritus
bridegroom, married man.

marriage bond
a document obtained by an engaged couple prior to their marriage. It affirmed that there was no moral or legal reason why the couple could not be married. In addition, the man affirmed that he would be able to support himself and his new bride.

marriage contract
legal agreement between prospective spouses made before marriage to determine their property rights and those of their children.

marriage records
a marriage record contains information about a marriage between two individuals. On a marriage record, you can at least find the bride's and groom's full names, the date of the marriage, and county where the marriage took place. Many marriage records include other information, such as the names and birthplace of the bride's and groom's parents, the addresses of the bride and groom, information about previous marriages, and the names of the witnesses to the marriage.

maternal line
line of descent traced through the mother's ancestry.

matron
older married woman with children.

mensis
month.

metes
measurements of distance in feet, rods, poles, chains, etc.; pertains to measuring direction and distance.

metes and bounds
method of surveying property by using physical and topographical features in conjunction with measurements.

mil. (abbreviation)
military.

military records
>   the US government has always kept records on all military and civilian workers. Most of these files have very detailed information, such as the individual's name, their spouse's name, date of birth, place of residence, which wars the individual served in, their military organisation (Navy, Marines, or Army), when the individual's service began and ended, where and when the individual died, and where the individual was buried.

militia
>   a citizen army; a military organisation formed by local citizens to serve in emergencies.

minor
>   a person under the legal age; historically, the legal age differed from place to place and over time. (Check prevailing law to determine the legal age requirement at a specific time).

mo. (abbreviation)
>   month.

mortality schedule
>   a section of the federal census listing information about persons who died during the census year.

mulatto
>   a mulatto is legally considered to be an individual with mixed Black and white heritage. However, some individuals who were designated mulattos may have a slightly more mixed parentage, perhaps including Native American blood.

naturalisation records
>   naturalisation records document the process by which an immigrant becomes a citizen. An individual has to live in the United States for a specific period of time and file a series of forms with a court before he or she can become naturalised. Naturalisation records provide the following information: place and date of birth, date of arrival into the United States, place of residence at the time of naturalisation, a personal description, and sometimes the name of the ship that the individual arrived on and the individual's occupation.

na. (abbrevation)
>   naturalised; not applicable.

natus
>   born.

n.d. (abbreviation)
>   no date; not dated.

nee
>   born, used to denote a woman's maiden name, i.e., Anne Gibson nee West.

n.p. (abbreviation)

no place listed; no publisher listed.

neph. (abbreviation)

nephew.

newspaper announcements

normally, newspapers announce events of genealogical interest such as births, deaths, and marriages. The amount of information in these announcements will vary. Most likely you will find the names of the individuals involved in the event, the date of the event, and where the event took place. Sometimes you can even find pictures.

nunc. (abbreviation)

nuncupative will, oral will.

nuncupative will

oral will declared or dictated by the testator in his last sickness before a sufficient number of witnesses and afterwards put in writing.

ob. (abbrevation)

obit, deceased.

OB (abbreviation)

order book, as in court order book.

obiit. (abbreviation)

he or she died.

obit. (abbreviation)

obituary.

octoroon

child of a quadroon; person having one-eighth Black ancestry.

of colour

Black, Indian, persons of mixed blood.

Old Dominion

Virginia.

old style calendar

Julian calendar, used before the Gregorian calendar.

olographic will

an olographic or holographic will is handwritten and signed by the individual that the will belongs to.

oral history

an oral history is a collection of family stories told by a member of the family or by a close family friend. Normally, an oral history is transcribed onto paper, or is video or tape recorded. Oral histories can yield some of the best information about a family – the kinds of things that you won't find written in records.

oral will

nuncupative will – oral will declared or dictated by the testator in his last sickness before a sufficient number of witnesses and afterwards put in writing.

orphan

a child whose mother, father, or both (usually) have died.

orphan asylum

an orphanage.

OS (abbreviation)

old style calendar.

Palatinate

area in Germany known as the Pfalz, Rheinland Pfalz and Bavarian Pfalz from which thousands of families immigrated to colonial America.

palaeography

study of handwriting.

parent county

the county from which a new county is formed.

parish

ecclesiastical division or jurisdiction; the site of a church.

passenger lists

lists of the names and information about passengers that arrived on ships into the United States. These lists were submitted to customs collectors at every port by the ship's master. Passenger lists were officially required by the United States government until 1820. Before that date, the information about each passenger varied widely, from names to number of bags.

patent

a government grant of property in fee simple to public lands; land grant.

paternal line

line of descent traced through the father's ancestry.

patronymics

the practice of creating last names from the name of one's father. For example, Robert, John's son, would become Robert Johnson. Robert Johnson's son Neil would become Neil Robertson.

pedigree

a person's ancestry, lineage, family tree.

pedigree chart

a chart showing a person's ancestry.

pension (military)

a benefit paid regularly to a person for military service or a military service related disability.

pensioner

person who receives pension benefits.

p.o.a. (abbreviation)

power of attorney.

poll

used in early tax records denoting a taxable person; person eligible to vote.

posthumous

a child born after the death of the father.

power of attorney

written instrument where one person, as principal, appoints someone as his or her agent, thereby authorising that person to perform certain acts on behalf of the principal, such as buying or selling property, settling an estate, representing them in court, etc.

pr. (abbreviation)

proved, probated.

p.r. (abbreviation)

parish register.

preponderance of evidence

evidence of greater weight or more convincing than the opposing evidence; evidence more credible and convincing, more reasonable and probable, and can be circumstantial in nature.

primary evidence

original or first-hand evidence; the best evidence available that must be used before secondary evidence can be introduced as proof.

primary source

primary sources are records that were created at the time of an event. For example, a primary source for a birth date would be a birth certificate. While you can find birth dates on other documents, such as marriage certificates, they would not be primary sources for the birth date, because they were not created at the time of the birth.

primogeniture

ensures the right of the eldest son to inherit the entire estate of his parents, to the exclusion of younger sons.

prob. (abbreviation)

probably; probated.

probate

legal process used to determine the validity of a will before the court authorises distribtion of an estate; legal process used to appoint someone to administer the estate of a deceased who did not leave a will.

probate records

records disposing of a deceased individual's property. They may include an individual's last will and testament, if one was made. The information you can get from probate records varies, but usually includes the name of the deceased, either the deceased's age at the time of death or birth date, property, members of the family, and the last place of residence.

progeniture
a direct ancestor.

public domain
land owned by a government.

Pvt. (abbreviation)
military rank of private.

quadroon
child of a mulatto and white parentage; a child with one Black grandparent.

quitclaim deed
transfer of land or claim without guaranteeing a clear title.

quit rent roll
in early Virginia, a list of those who paid the annual fee to the King in exchange for the right to live on and farm property.

quod vide
directs the reader to look in another part of the book for further information.

q.v. (abbreviation)
quod vide (see above).

R.C. (abbreviation)
Roman Catholic.

real property
land and anything attached to it, such as houses, building, barns, growing timber, growing crops, etc.

rec'd (abbreviation)
received.

receiver
person appointed by court to hold property until a suit is settled.

reconveyance
property sold to another person is transferred back to the original owner.

reeve
churchwarden; early name for sheriff in England.

reg. (abbreviation)
register.

relicta
widow.

relictus
widower.

relict
> widow.

repud. (abbreviation)
> repudiate.

res. (abbreviation)
> residence; research.

researcher ID card
> All researchers using original records at the National Archives or National Archives regional centres must get a researcher ID card. If you just plan to use microfilmed records, you do not need to get an ID card. To get an ID card you will be asked to fill out an application. You should bring photo identification, such as a driver's licence, school identification card, or passport on your first visit to the archives. Researcher ID cards are free of charge and are valid for two years. The ID card must be presented at each visit.

ret. (abbreviation)
> retired.

Rev. (abbreviation)
> reverend.

Rev. War (abbreviation)
> Revolutionary War.

rustica
> country girl.

rusticus
> country boy.

s. (abbreviation)
> son.

s. & h. (abbreviation)
> son and heir.

secondary evidence
> evidence that is inferior to primary evidence or the best evidence.

secondary source
> a secondary source is a record that was created a significant amount of time after an event occurred. For example, a marriage certificate would be a secondary source for a birth date, because the birth took place several years before the time of the marriage. However, that same marriage certificate would be a primary source for a marriage date, because it was created at the time of the marriage.

self-addressed stamped envelope (sase)
> when you request records or other information from people and institutions, you should include a self-addressed stamped envelope (SASE) in your letter. Of course, an SASE with U.S. postage stamps

on it is only good in the United States. If you are expecting return mail from overseas, you should include an International Reply Coupon with your self-addressed envelope. This coupon serves as payment for any international postage you many need to pay. They can be purchased at your local post office.

serv. (abbreviation)

servant.

sibling

a brother or sister, persons who share the same parents in common.

sic

Latin term signifying a copy reads exactly as the original; incicates a possible mistake in the original.

s/o

son of.

soc. (abbreviation)

society.

Social Security Death Index

the Social Security Death Index is an index of Social Security Death records. Generally this includes names of deceased Social Security recipients whose relatives applied for Social Security Death Benefits after their passing. Also included in the millions of records are approximately 400,000 railroad retirement records from the early 1900s to 1950s.

Soundex

phonetic indexing system.

source

the document, record, publication, manuscript, etc. used to prove a fact.

sponsor

an individual other than the parents of a child who takes responsibility for the child's religious education. Sponsors are usually present at a child's baptism. Sponsors are often referred to as godparents.

srnm. (abbreviation)

surname, last name.

St. (abbreviation)

saint; street.

statute

a law enacted by Government. Excludes 'common law'.

step

used in conjunction with a degree of kinship.

stepchild

child of one of the spouses by a former marriage who has not been adopted by the step-parent.

stepfather
> husband of a child's mother by a later marriage.

stepmother
> wife of a child's father by a later marriage.

surg. (abbreviation)
> surgeon.

surname
> last name, family name.

T. (abbreviation)
> township.

terr. (abbreviation)
> territory.

test. (abbreviation)
> testament.

testate
> died leaving a valid will.

testis
> witness.

testator
> man who writes a valid will.

testatrix
> woman who writes a valid will.

tithable
> a person taxable by law.

tithe
> in English law, the tenth part of one's annual income paid to support noblemen and clergy; amount of annual poll tax.

township
> in a government survey, is a square tract six miles on each side containing thirty-six square miles of land; a name given to the civil and political subdivisons of a county.

twp (an abbreviation)
> township.

ultimo
> the preceding month.

unk. (abbreviation)
> unknown.

unprobated will
> will never submitted for probate.

unsolemn will
> will in which an executor is not named.

unm. (abbreviation)
> unmarried.

uxor.
> wife, spouse, consort.

valid
> that which is legal and binding.

vestry
> administrative group within a parish; the ruling body of a church.

vidua
> widow.

viduus
> widower.

virgo
> used to describe an unmarried woman in English and European marriage records.

vital records
> birth, marriage, and death records.

warranty deed
> guarantees a clear property title from the seller to the buyer.

wheelwright
> person who makes and repairs vehicle wheels, such as carts, wagons, etc.

widow
> a widow is a woman whose husband has died.

widower
> a widower is a man whose wife has died.

witness
> a witness is an individual present at an event such as a marriage or the signing of a document who can vouch that the event took place.

white rent
> blackmail; rent to be paid in silver.

will
> a document stating how a person wants real and personal property divided after death.

writ of attachment
> court order authorising the seizure of property sufficient to cover debts and court costs for not appearing in court.

writ of summons
> document ordering a person to appear in court.

yeoman
> farmer; freeholder who works a small estate; rank below gentleman.

Appendix 6

COMPUTERS IN GENEALOGY
SOCIETY OF GENEALOGISTS QUARTERLY MAGAZINE
ARTICLES AND REVIEWS IN BACK NUMBERS 1997–1999

Articles

- **Area-specific genealogy mailing lists,** by Mark Howells [6.3]
- **Belling the Cat: Certifying Genealogical Software,** by George Archer [6.2]
- **Brief survey of family history society Web sites** by Brian Randall & Iain Kerr [6.7]
- **Certifying genealogy software: a discussion** between Barney Tyrwhitt-Drake & George Archer [6.3]
- **Character sets for genealogists,** by Barney Tyrwhitt-Drake [6.10]
- *CiG* **Reader Survey,** by Ian Philpot [6.3]
- **Customizable genealogical software,** by Vivienne Dunstan [6.4]
- **Diagrams & charts for genealogy: an introduction to VISIO** by Martin Vlietstra [6.6]
- **Digital cameras in genealogy – gimmick or godsend?,** by Barney Tyrwhitt-Drake [6.9]
- **Don Francis FSG – An Appreciation,** by Eric D Probert [6.2]
- **Experiences of running an e-mail list for a Family History Society,** by Phil Stringer [6.3]
- **The Future of Internet Genealogy – twelve predictions,** by Mark Howells [6.9]
- **Genealogical Software When Storage-Space Is At A Premium,** by Martin & Vivienne Dunstan [6.1]
- **Genealogy & Family History Shareware Programmes,** by Eric D Probert [6.1]
- **Genealogy & the Search Engines** by Peter Christian [6.12]
- **Genealogy Software** by Eric D Probert [6.6]
- **Genet's Genealogical Data Model** by David Squire [6.11]
- **Getting the most from FamilySearch,** by Bryan Grant [6.10]
- **Getting the SoG Bookshop on-line** by Barney Tyrwhitt-Drake [6.7]
- **IGI Downloads in PAF 3.0 format (GEDCOM 5.5),** by David Hawgood [6.5]
- **Link rot in your family tree? A Case Study in the Dynamics of Internet Genealogy** by Mark Howells [6.8]
- **Mailing List Basics,** by Peter Christian [6.3]

- **The Millennium Bug – what does it mean for family historians?** by Barney Tyrwhitt-Drake [6.6]
- **Non-Windows Genealogy Software,** by Eric D Probert [6.10]
- **A novel representation of parish neighbourhoods** by Martin Vlietstra [6.7]
- **The paperless genealogist** – using a palmtop by Barney Tyrwhitt-Drake [6.11]
- **Perfecting Pedigree – a model for other programs?** by Philip Richards [6.8]
- **Portable computing for genealogy with Windows CE** by David Frost [6.8]
- **A portable scanning solution for genealogists? – the HP CapShare** by Barney Tyrwhitt-Drake [6.12]
- **Recording legacies in a linked database,** by Philip Richards [6.10]
- **The presentation of genealogical information using HTML** by John Bending [6.6]
- **Society of Genealogists mailing lists** by Geoffrey Stone [6.7]
- **The Society of Genealogists On-line,** by Peter Christian [6.5]
- **The Society's library catalogue project** by John Addis-Smith [6.7]
- **Soundex – can it be improved?,** by Peter Christian [6.5]
- **Soundex – one way of looking for surname variants,** by Barney Tyrwhitt-Drake [6.5]
- **Soundex Update** by Peter Christian [6.6]
- **Symposium Report: Advances in Genealogical Computing,** by David Hawgood [6.4]
- **A system of cross-referencing data** by John Bending [6.12]
- **Turning IGI Data into Information,** by Barney Tyrwhitt-Drake [6.1]
- **The 2% sample of the 1851 UK census revisited,** by Barney Tyrwhitt-Drake [6.2]
- **Updating the Victorian Pioneers Index** by Faye Guthrie [6.8]
- **Using a database for transcribing the 1891 census,** by Barney Tyrwhitt-Drake [6.4]
- **Using the 1881 Census CD-ROM** by Stephen Archer [6.11]
- **What Is A 'Personal Computer'?,** by Harvey Nyman [6.1]
- **Windows Genealogy Software,** by Eric D Probert [6.5]
- **Windows Genealogy Software,** by Eric D Probert [6.9]

Software Reviews

- *1851 UK Census 2% Extract* (S&N) reviewed by Peter Christian [6.4]
- *The Biographical Database 1680–1830 Personal Research Edition*, reviewed by Peter Christian [6.2]

- **BIRDIE,** reviewed by Dennis Clarke [6.2]
- **Custodian** [Windows], published by P & S Smith, reviewed by David Hawgood [6.7]
- **Family Treemaker for the PCW,** reviewed by Ken Drake [6.3]
- **Frith's Photographic Directory. Volume 1: Great Britain and Ireland,** published by The Francis Frith Collection, reviewed by Peter Christian [6.8]
- **Geneal** a genealogical data display system for PostScript, reviewed by Christopher Barham [6.9]
- *The Genealogical Research Directory (GRD) on CD-ROM,* reviewed by Peter Christian [6.1]
- **Generations de Luxe Family Tree Software** [Windows], published by Sierra On-line, reviewed by Roland Clare [6.7]
- **Generations Grande Suite,** published by Sierra, reviewed by Roland Clare [6.9]
- **GENI: GEDCOM viewer for the Psion 3,** reviewed by Ken Clarke [6.2]
- *Index to Griffiths Valuation of Ireland 1848–1864,* published by Genealogical Publishing Co./Broderbund, reviewed by Barney Tyrwhitt-Drake [6.7]
- *Irish Census 1831, 1841* (Broderbund) reviewed by Barney Tyrwhitt-Drake [6.4]
- **Legacy** [Windows] Published by Millennium, reviewed by Roland Clare [6.6]
- **Personal Ancestral File 4.0,** reviewed by Iain Kerr [6.11]
- **Personal Ancestral File 4.0,** update to the review in the previous issue, by Iain Kerr [6.12]
- **Pigot's 1830 Directory of Berkshire, Buckinghamshire and Oxfordshire on CD-ROM,** Published by Drake Software Associates, reviewed by Malcolm Austen [6.9]
- **Tri-County CD** (S&N) images of Devon, Norfolk and Warwickshire churches, reviewed by Peter Christian [6.10]
- **Ultimate Family Tree** [Windows] reviewed by Ian Care [6.6]
- *Your Heritage, Your Family?,* published by Hurst Village Publishing, reviewed by Peter Christian [6.7]

Book Reviews

- Marthe Arends *Genealogy Software Guide,* published by Genealogical Software Company, reviewed by Peter Christian [6.9]
- Peter Christian, *Web Publishing for Genealogy,* reviewed by David Squire [6.1]
- Peter Christian, *Web Publishing for Genealogy,* 2nd ed., reviewed by Iain Kerr [6.12]

- John & Carolyn Cosgriff, *Turbo Technology. An Introduction to Family History Reserach in the Information Age*, reviewed by Peter Christian [6.3]
- Elizabeth Powell Crowe, *Genealogy Online. Researching Your Roots* reviewed by Peter Christian [6.4]
- David Hawgood, *Computer Genealogy Update*, reviewed by Peter Christian [6.1]
- David Hawgood, *Gedcom Data Transfer – moving your family tree*, reviewed by Stephen Archer [6.12]
- Matthew L Helm & April Leigh Helm, *Genealogy On-line for Dummies* published by IDG Books, reviewed by Peter Christian [6.8]
- Joe Houghton, *Making More of Brothers Keeper for Windows*, reviewed by Alan Lindfield [6.1]
- Cyndi Howells, *Netting Your Ancestors. Genealogical Research on the Internet* reviewed by Peter Christian [6.4]
- Cyndi Howells, *Cyndi's List*, reviewed by Peter Christian [6.12]
- Thomas Jay Kemp, *Virtual Roots. A Guide to Genealogy and Local History on the World Wide Web*, reviewed by Eric D Probert [6.3]
- Christina K Schaefer, *A Genealogist's No-Frills Guide to British Isles (Instant Information on the Internet)*, reviewed by Peter Christian [6.12]
- Roy Stockhill, *Family History Newsletters From the Desktop*, reviewed by David Hawgood [6.4]
- Phil Young, *Computers for Genealogy. A guide*, reviewed by Peter Christian [6.3]

Index